D1614875

# The Flesh of Words

THE LIBRARY
UNIVERSITY OF
WINCHESTER
KA 0388241

PHILOSOPHY   POLITICAL THEORY   AESTHETICS

*Judith Butler and Frederick M. Dolan*

EDITORS

UNIVERSITY OF WINCHESTER
LIBRARY

UNIVERSITY OF WINCHESTER
LIBRARY

# The Flesh of Words

THE POLITICS OF WRITING

*Jacques Rancière*

Translated by Charlotte Mandell

Stanford University Press

Stanford, California

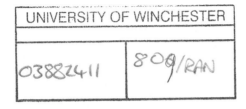

UNIVERSITY OF WINCHESTER

03882411    809/RAN

Stanford University Press
Stanford, California

This book has been published with the assistance of the
French Ministry of Culture—National Center for the Book.

No part of this book may be reproduced or transmitted in any form or by any
means, electronic or mechanical, including photocopying and recording, or in any
information storage or retrieval system without the prior written permission of
Stanford University Press.

English translation © 2004 by the Board of Trustees of the
Leland Stanford Junior University. All rights reserved.

*The Flesh of Words* was originally published in French in 1998 under the title
*La chair des mots: Politiques de l'écriture* © 1998, Éditions Galilée.

Printed in the United States of America
on acid-free, archival-quality paper.

Library of Congress Cataloging-in-Publication Data

Rancière, Jacques.
　[Chair des mots. English]
　The flesh of words : the politics of writing / Jacques Rancière ;
translated by Charlotte Mandell.
　　　p.　cm. — (Atopia)
　Includes bibliographical references.
　ISBN 0-8047-4078-x (pbk : alk. paper)
　ISBN 0-8047-4069-0 (cloth : alk. paper)
1. Literature—History and criticism.　I. Title.　II. Series: Atopia
(Stanford, Calif.)
PN513 .R3613 2004
809—DC22

2003025734

Original Printing 2004

Last figure below indicates year of this printing:
13　12　11

Typeset by Tim Roberts in 11/14 Adobe Garamond

# Contents

## Translator's Note

All quotations from European literary texts have been translated directly from the French as cited by Jacques Rancière. Thus quotations from Rimbaud, Mallarmé, Proust, Balzac, Flaubert, Deleuze and Althusser are translated anew, while texts originally in other languages (Mandelstam, Auerbach) are translated here from the French and compared with existing translations where these exist. Texts that began life as English poems (Wordsworth, Byron, Shelley) have been restored to their original form.

A note is needed on that celebrated polychrest, the word *écrire* and its derivatives. This ordinary word for 'to write' produces the word *écriture*, which means both writing (in the most active or the most general sense) but also Scripture, in the sense of the Holy Scriptures. Rancière plays extensively on these overlapping meanings.

It is my pleasant obligation to acknowledge, with great gratitude, the guidance I received from the author, who carefully read and annotated the draft of my translation, and, after a memorable lecture he gave at Bard College in April 2003, generously discussed with me a few points that needed clarification. I wish also to thank many friends and colleagues who helped me with information, interpretation, nuance or guidance, especially Odile Chilton, Marina van Zuylen, John Yau, Olivier Brossard, Yan Brailowsky, Éric Trudel, Catherine Liu, Peter Krapp, Pierre Joris, Nicole Peyrafitte, my husband, Robert Kelly, and the staff of the Stevenson Library at Bard College.

The Flesh of Words

# The Excursions of the Word

"In the beginning was the Word." It is not the beginning that is difficult, the affirmation of the Word that is God and the assertion of his incarnation. It is the end. Not because it's missing from the Gospel of John, but because there are two, each of which says that there are still an infinite number of things to say, an infinite number of signs to reveal, which go to prove that the Word did indeed become flesh. Criticism has, it's true, declared that the second ending of the Gospel is apocryphal. In a coarse style, the narrative relates a new apparition of Jesus at Tiberias and a new miraculous fishing expedition, in a strangely vivid, popular tone: Peter dives into the lake to rejoin the Savior, who has appeared on the shore, and the apostles find a little campfire on the shore that is both a brazier to grill fish and also the Light that has come down into the world. It is as if, to bring his book to completion, the author had to make the great story of the Incarnate Word pass into all the little stories of the everyday labors of the people. As if he had also to assure the passage of the witness, of the Incarnate Word, into sacred writing, from the Scriptures [*Écritures*] to writing [*écriture*], from writing to the world, which is its destination. After a triple question posed by Jesus to Peter, which corresponds to the three cock crows, and renders legitimacy to the head of the Church, the text ends by testifying that its compiler is indeed the disciple chosen by Jesus to relate the deeds of the embodiment of the Word. The critics are probably right: the demonstration is too obvious not to have been added on. But the important thing is precisely that this addition was necessary, that the first ending straightaway required a second one, which unrolls its logic and transforms its symbolic function into a prosaic narrative: to insure the passage from the subject of the Book to the narrator of the story, to project the book toward a reality that is not the one it speaks of, but the one in which it must become a deed, a power of life.

Thus the flaw is revealed at the moment of saying goodbye to the Word made flesh and sending its book into the world, at the instant of letting writing say all by itself what the Sacred Writings say. An entire tradition of thinking and writing has nonetheless been nourished by the example of the Book par excellence, the book of the Word made flesh, the ending that returns to the beginning, the two testaments folded in on each other: romantic bibles of the nations or of humanity; books of our century skillfully constructed according to the game that comes full circle. How many books have been dreamt of following this model of coincidence, how many have been created only for the sake of their last sentence, for the glorious rhyme it makes with the first! But the over-easy confidence in the virtues of the book closed in on itself encounters, under another form, the paradox of the ending. The difficult thing is not to stop the book. It is not the last sentence that poses a problem, but the next-to-last. It is not the void into which the finished book must throw itself, but the space that separates it from its end and allows the end to come. Balzac the writer of newspaper serials has already given *Le curé de village* [The village priest] its ending. Balzac the novelist, however, will need two years and two hundred more pages to catch up with that ending. The conclusion of *Le temps retrouvé* [Time regained] was conceived at the same time as the beginning of *Du côté de chez Swann* [Swann's way] in 1908. No doubt Proust revised the "Perpetual Adoration" in the Library and the "*Bal de têtes*" that follows it in the salon many times. But a strange distance has taken shape on the path that leads there. A war that the novelist could not foresee had to happen, and one hundred and fifty supplementary pages for the book to reach the end, from which it had begun. And in this space that separates Véronique Graslin [a character in Balzac's *The Village Priest*—Trans.] from her death, or the Proustian narrator from revelation, it is not the void that threatens but rather, as we shall see, the risk of an overabundance, the clash of a truth made flesh that can overwhelm the fragile truth of the book.

So a strange game is played between words and their body. Since Plato and the *Cratylus* it has been understood that words do not resemble what they say. That is the price of thought. Any resemblance must be resisted. But, by identifying this resemblance with the poetic lie, Plato gave himself too easy a task. For poetry and fiction have the same demand. That is what Mallarmé says, correcting his cratylian reveries of an amateur philologist with the poet's rigor. If chance had not made the very sound of *nuit* [night] light and that of *jour* [day] dark, verse would not exist, which rewards the faults of language, and makes only the absent one of all flowers rise up.

But doesn't this condemnation of resemblance, which modern poetry has inherited from ancient philosophy, itself settle the question too quickly? For there are many ways of imitating, and many things that can be resembled. And when it was said that sound did not resemble meaning, or that a sentence was like no object in the world, only the most obvious of the doors through which words can go toward what are not words has been closed. And the least essential, too. For it is not by describing that words acquire their power: it is by naming, by calling, by commanding, by intriguing, by seducing that they slice into the naturalness of existences, set humans on their path, separate them and unite them into communities. The word has many other things to imitate besides its meaning or its referent: the power of speech that brings it into existence, the movement of life, the gestures of an oration, the effect it anticipates, the addressee whose listening or reading it mimics beforehand: "Take, read!", "Reader, throw away this book." If resemblance in painting is denounced, isn't that because it fixes all movements on one single plane? That indeed is what the criticism of [Plato's] *Phaedrus* definitively tells us when it denounces the vain portrayal of *logos* presented by the silent letters of the script. The problem is not that the resemblance is unfaithful, but that it is too faithful, still attached to what has been said when already it should be elsewhere, near where the meaning of what has been said must speak. The written letter is like a silent painting that retains on its body the movements that animate the logos and bring it to its destination. The chattering silence of the dead letter blocks the multiple powers by which the *logos* constitutes its theater, imitates itself to perform living speech, to travel the path of its oration, to become seed able to bear fruit in the soul of the disciple. And the entire text of *Phaedrus* is only the deployment of all the luxuries by which writing exceeds itself in the mime of living speech, of speech on the march that traverses all the figures of discourse in movement: walking around, dialogue, debate, parody, myth, oracle, prayer.

This is the theater that will be at issue here, the way a text gives itself the body of its incarnation to escape the fate of the letter released into the world, to mime its own movement between the place of thought, of mind, of life, whence it comes, and the place toward which it heads: a sort of human theater where speech [*parole*] becomes action, takes possession of souls, leads bodies and gives rhythm to their walk. It will be a question of that superior imitation by which language tries to escape the deceptions of imitation. The theater initiated by Socrates' stroll and Phaedrus' walk is really that of the excursions [*sorties*] of the word. But there are good and bad excursions. As to the bad, a fine example is those catastrophic "excursions" of Don Quixote, the man who wants to complete the book and believes that this consists of finding resemblances to the book in reality. And then there are the good excursions, the ones that refuse to crash against the walls hurling themselves in front of images, and thus apply themselves to erasing the separation that is the correlative to mimetic prestige. So it is a matter of finding, like Plato, beneath words and resemblances, the power by which words are set in motion and become deeds. Thus the young Wordsworth, while reading Cervantes, dreams of a world where the mind could leave an imprint of itself in an element all its own, as close as possible to its own nature. But if he dreams in this way, it is, of course, because he is the contemporary of that French Revolution that claimed to lead a few old words back to their original power, words like liberty, equality, or nation, to make them the song of a people on the march. With that revolution begins the dream of which Rimbaud gave the most dazzling version: that of a poetry that resounds with the "new harmony," whose footstep makes "the new man rise up and march" [*Illuminations*, "For a Reason," trans. W. Fowlie]. But there also begins the conflict of poetry with itself. It asserts its freedom and separates itself from the prose of the world only at the cost of making itself like a music of bodies on their way toward the reign of the Spirit or the New Man, toward a truth possessed in a soul and body where it loses itself. And its work is then to cast aside its own utopia, at the risk of withdrawing itself from language, of putting the key under the door, like Rimbaud, or of making itself, like Mandelstam, the "oblivion of the word" it was about to utter.

Thus is defined a singular relationship between literature, philosophy, and politics, of which Althusser and Deleuze are the witnesses here. In the work of Althusser, the philosopher tries to condemn the "religious myth of the Book" and distinguish the reality unique to thought from all "lived reality." And this preoccupation seems to agree precisely with the rigor of the intellectual communist, anxious to escape the fate of quixotic well-intentioned souls. But it is exactly this conjunction that contains the flaw, imposes theater and its exit [*sortie*] as models of the passage from text to reality, and creates a dramaturgy of writing in which the resources of typography transpose the movements of Socrates and his disciple into the effect anticipated by their speech. As for Deleuze, he makes his entire philosophy a challenge of the mimetic figure of thought whose father is Plato, the accuser of the evil *mimesis*. And his analysis of works of literature contrasts the pure materiality of the formula with the mirages of representation. But the formula is both of those things: it is the pure play of language and it is the magic word that opens doors. But the door that Deleuze charges literature with opening is, like Althusser, that of a people still to come. Thus Bartleby the human formula becomes a mythological figure of filiation and finally identifies himself with the mediator above all others, the one who opened the gates of Rimbaud's "ancient hell," the son of the Word or the Word incarnate, "the Christ or brother of us all."

The relationship between literature and philosophy in connection with politics seems to function in reverse. Philosophy, which wants to separate its language from all the glamour of mimesis and its effect from all "literary" vacuity, does so only at the price of uniting with the most radical forms by which literature mimics the incarnation of the word. With these mad sorties of philosophy our era readily contrasts the wisdom of literature, separating the solitude of words and the pure chance of their encounters from the philosophical and political mirages of incarnation. But this wisdom is not linked to some more original conception of the nature of language, or to some more lucid view of the communal incarnation of the word. It is rather a logic of perseverance in its being. Literature lives only by the separation of words in relation to any body that might incarnate their power. It lives only by evading the incarnation that it incessantly puts into play. That is the paradox Balzac runs up against when in a novel he denounces the evil that novels produce, and when he discovers that the only solution to evil, "good" writing, imposes silence on the novelist. It is the paradox that Proust resolves, when he encounters in the epic of the nation at war a radical symbol of incarnate truth. To this truth made flesh which takes its own truth away from fiction, he responds with the sacrilegious passion that nails onto the "rock of pure matter" not only the aesthete Charlus but the very Spirit that bears words to prove itself by becoming living flesh. And of course this final struggle, which gives discourse and fiction their own truth, must always be begun anew (1). Against all nihilist wisdom, we will insist that is what makes it worth it.

PART I

*The Politics of the Poem*

# ONE

# From Wordsworth to Mandelstam:
# The Transports of Liberty

Under the rubric "poets' politics," we don't mean the opinions, experiences and political involvements of this or that poet; nor do we mean the reception or political interpretation of this or that text. The question that interests us here is the following: what essential necessity links the modern stance of poetic utterance with that of political subjectivity? Let us start with a simple example, borrowed from the most famous poem in the English language, William Wordsworth's "Daffodils": how does the "I" that is present in it, the "I" of "I wandered lonely as a cloud," have to do with the history of revolutionary subjectivity, whatever the well-attested versatility of the poet's political opinions and the equally attested political indifference of the daffodils may be?

Of course, the example is not a simple example. The solitary walker is already an established figure of literary subjectivity and modern politics. And the "I" that is identified in this poem has as its double the "I" of manifesto: for instance, the 1802 preface to *Lyrical Ballads* in which Wordsworth vindicates and defines for an entire era a subjective revolution of poetic writing.

But the emancipation of lyricism cannot consist simply of shaking off the dust of obsolete rules and the pomp of conventional expressions. It does not concern first the object of the poem and the means given to the poet. It concerns first of all the subject of the poem, the "I" of lyrical utterance. To emancipate lyricism means to liberate this "I" from a certain politics of writing. For in the old canons, the ones that separated poetic genres, their own rules and their respective dignity were clearly political. And the question can be posed thus: isn't a new form of political experience necessary to emancipate the lyrical subject from the old poetic-political framework?

## The Place of Lyricism

The question posed here ties in with a discussion that has proved to be a determining one for modern thinking on poetics: it deals with the exact origin and significance of the division of poetic genres. We know that many contemporary authors have wondered about the tripartition of the tragic, the epic, and the lyric, about the way—done entirely retrospectively—in which this triad was formed in the Romantic era and on the false filiation that sought to attach it to the distinctions in Plato's *Republic* and Aristotle's *Poetics*. They observed that the lyrical genre is absent in Aristotle and that one can find it in Plato only at the price of identifying it with the "simple narration," cited in Book III of the *Republic* as proper to the dithyramb. They noted that the works praised by posterity as exemplary of Greek lyricism, those of Sappho or Pindar for instance, have no place in the distinctions of the two philosophers. In Plato as in Aristotle, the division between the different types of poems is in fact made according to two dividing lines that, on one hand, do not define "genres" and, on the other, do not recognize the lyric as a species differentiated by a pertinent trait. These two dividing lines are first the nature of the represented, second the method of utterance (1).

The nature of the represented is the quality of the characters represented by the poem: the more or less elevated status of their identity and the conformity or non-conformity of their actions with this status. It is on this basis that Plato denounces the epic when it falsely represents the gods, or tragedy when it presents heroes torn apart by passion and moaning wretchedly about their fate. It is also from this point of view that—in a less moralizing and more soberly classifying register—Aristotle distinguishes tragedy and epic, which represent noble characters, from comedy and parody, which represent ordinary people.

The method of utterance—the Platonic *lexis*—is the way in which the poet as subject relates to the subject of the poem, identifies with it, differentiates himself from it or hides himself behind it. It is on this basis that Plato distinguishes the deceptive *mimesis* of the tragic, which attributes its discourse to the characters in the play, the supposedly pure and non-deceiving narrative of the dithyramb, and the mixture of *mimesis* and narrative proper to the epic, in which the poet sometimes tells the story in his own voice, sometimes mimics the speech of his characters.

Thus the question of the status of the poem is not first of all a question of division into genres. The "quality" of the poem is not defined by common genus and species differences. It depends on the encounter between a way of speaking—a way of posing or eliding the "I" of the poet—and a way of representing, or not representing, people "as they should be," in the double sense of the expression: people who are as it is fitting they should be, and who are represented as it is fitting to represent them. The enduring lesson of Platonic conceptualization is this: there is no pure poetics. Poetry is an art of composing fables that represent characters and act upon characters. It thus belongs to a political experience of the physical: to the relationship between the *nomoi* of the city—the laws that reign there, but also the songs that are sung—and the *ethos* of the citizens—their character, but also their humor. Poetics is from the beginning political. It is so by the conjunction between a certain type of individual that should or should not be imitated and a certain place of utterance that is or is not suitable to what must be the *tone* of the city.

We see now why the lyric poem does not have to be specified within this schema. The poetic forms in it can be made out and examined as they link a certain kind of *lexis* to a certain kind of representation. The place of lyricism is an empty place in this schema, that of un-signifying poetry, inoffensive because it is non-representational and because it does not pose or hide any distancing between the poet-subject and the subject of the poem. The unambiguous "I" of the lyric poem cannot pose a problem to the "we" of the community, whereas tragedy splits it in two by the deception of the *lexis*, and the epic corrupts it by the falsification of the *muthos*. Good poetry is equivalent to a non-poetry that does not fabricate any lie and does not divide any subject.

We also see how modernity can pose again the question of lyricism (and eventually invent a genealogy for it): on one hand, modern poetry fills precisely that "empty" place of a non-representational poetry, and consequently seeks to challenge any allegiance to a philosophic-political test of the representation/enunciation nexus. But oversimplifying this contrast might neutralize another form of "allegiance" or political membership, might both presuppose and negate a political experience of the poem unique to the age of modern revolutions. This experience could be thought of as a reorganization of the relationship between the three terms of the ancient poetic-political system: the status of representation, the opposition of high and low, the relationship between the poet subject and the subject of the poem. Modern lyricism could thus be thought of not primarily as an experience of self or a discovery of nature or sensibility, but as a new political experience of the physical world, or a physical experience of politics.

So we can say in short: the modern lyric revolution is not a way of experiencing oneself, of experiencing the profundity of one's inner life, or, conversely, of immersing it in the profundity of nature. It is primarily a specific method of utterance, a way of accompanying one's saying, of deploying it in a perceptual space, of giving it rhythm in a walk, a journey, a crossing. Wind, clouds, the path or the wave, which hold a well-known place in Romantic poetry, are not first of all the drunken experience of wild nature; they are first operators of accompaniment—methods that allow the "I" to slip its way throughout the poem until it makes itself the space of the appearance of daffodils "in person."

*Accompaniment* means several things: firstly, the question of lyricism emerges when poetry becomes aware of itself as the act of accompanying itself, as the ability of the "I" to coexist with its saying (whether or not the poem is in the first person), that is to say a certain way for the poet to constitute himself and to be his likeness, his brother, Baudelaire's "hypocrite" reader, alone in an echo-chamber with his song. But this "I" that accompanies the poem and that is produced in echo with its act is also the subjectivity of a traveler who passes through a certain territory, makes words coincide with things, utterances with visions, and implicates in this travel some relationship with the "we" of the community. Between the "I" of "I wandered lonely as a cloud" and the first person plural of "Allons Enfants de la patrie!" [Let us go, Children of the homeland—the opening line of the "Marseillaise"—Trans.] there is an essential relationship that is not only the resemblance between the two stories about going and the two armies—of patriots and of daffodils—but that also affects the way in which the "I" of the poet relates to the cloud of the poem in the manner of the *as* of metaphor, of a self-canceling metaphor that comes to contrast with the *as if* of *mimesis*. The relationship of the "I" to the cloud is withdrawn from any act of mimetic fabulation. The function of the metaphor is precisely identified with what its etymology signifies: that of transport—even if it means that this function varies according to whether it is the simple accompaniment that links the subject to his cloud, or is the patriotic transport that links children to their new mother.

So enunciative accompaniment is in league with a problematic of metaphor as transport. The method of subjectification and figuration unique to the lyric poem comes to be grafted onto other methods of figuration and subjectification in which politics, in the revolutionary age, also assumes new figures: for instance, the geographic and symbolic representation of the nation, the territorial journey of the traveler—especially of the pedestrian traveler—the practice of vision using sketches and sketchbooks. . . . The subjectivity proper to the lyric poem involves the displacement of a body onto a landscape, in a coincidence of vision and word, which constitutes this territory as the space of writing. It is this manner of territorialization, of making present to the senses, which doubly undermines the old model of the politics of the poem: on one hand, it suppresses the distancing of *mimesis*; on the other, it annuls any division between high and low, noble and base. It creates the possibility for the poet to withdraw from the duty of representation, to wander "like a cloud," with the clouds. And this possibility has a name, uttered in the thirty-first of the eight thousand lines of William Wordsworth's *Prelude*: "Dear Liberty," an English poetic translation of the French political *Liberté chérie*.

So I will explore the following hypothesis: the liberty that shaped the modern poetic revolution is a way the poet has of accompanying his utterance [*dit*]. This accompaniment has as its condition of possibility a new political experiment of the sensory, a new way politics has of making itself felt and of affecting the *ethos* of the citizen in the age of modern revolutions. For politics, in the modern era, has come to dwell in the very place which was for Plato or Aristotle the non-signifying, the non-representative. The modern system of political representation is based on a non-representative figuration that precedes it, an immediate visibility of meaning [*sens*] in the sensory. The fundamental axis of the poetic-political relationship is thus not the one where the "truth" of the utterance depends on the "quality" of what is represented. It rests in the method of presentation, in the way in which utterance makes itself present, imposes the recognition of immediate meaning in the sensory.

Lyricism is a political experiment of the sensory, but it is also a polemical experiment, in a double sense. First, it is the form of writing that knows that it must face the sensory writing of the political, the immediate figurability of politics in the order of sensory presentation, and thus confronted with a certain political *transport* and constrained to turn away from it. The modern poetic revolution tests its connection with political transport and experiences the tension of a necessary deflection. It tests the necessity of retracing, redrawing the line of passage that separates and unites words and things. That is certainly the solid core of what has been expressed, especially in Eastern Europe, about the function of resistance in poetry. The lyric revolution is the effort to undo a necessary and untenable connection with the battles of revolutionary or counterrevolutionary politics.

But perhaps the modern lyric—and this is the second aspect of its "polemics"—achieves the purity of its progress only at the price of forgetting the metaphorical journey that makes it possible. The fortunate lyric encounter between the "I," words and things, presupposes a preliminary trip, a reconnaissance trip, a trip that assures the possibility of reconnaissance. The "reconnaissance trip" relates to an exemplary procedure for the production of meaning, the metaphor, and to an exemplary poetic form, the epic. Modern lyricism asserts itself in a unique relationship with the epic, defied or denied, forgotten or re-conceived. Behind the lyric *wandering*, there is a Greek journey, an erased and reinterpreted odyssey. But Ulysses' journey is also the journey of the deceiver or the traitor. And lyricism is then called to return to the place of the lie or of the original treason by which meaning exists, the meaning that sings itself.

My account will be organized, then, like a journey between four poles, or four journeys. Beginning with the question of an initial walk—what permits this *wandering* [English in original—Trans.] of the "I" toward the *daffodils* like a cloud and with the clouds?—I will try to show that it presupposes another pedestrian journey, in revolutionary France, which in turn presupposes a preliminary journey to the Greek place of metaphor, which then implies a final journey to the Trojan place of treason. The journey between four poles will also be the journey from one revolution—the French—to another, the Russian, from one agent of metaphoricity—Wordsworth's cloud—to another—the swallow of Mandelstam's poems, those poems that seem to me to close an age of poets' politics, by poetically constructing the whole system of political metaphoricity of modern lyricism; these poems, which wonder obstinately about the presence, in the present time, of Petersburg—the city of stone—and of the wood of the Achaean ships and Horse at the siege of Troy, the presence of an *immemorial* to the treason at the origin of words that the lyric poet makes coincide with the joy of an unexpected spectacle: armies of daffodils, or proletarians attacking heaven.

> The Achaeans in darkness prepare the horse
> Firmly, toothed saws dig deep into the walls
> And nothing can calm the dry rumor of blood
> And for you there is no name, no sound, no imprint.
> —Osip Mandelstam, "Because I did not know . . . "

## The Cloud Companion

In the beginning, there is name, sound, and imprint: the name, sound and imprint of liberty as, on July 14, 1790, the day of the great revolutionary Feast of the Federation, William Wordsworth encounters them on his way to the Alps, in accordance with the basic principle of his politics of the journey:

> . . . and should the chosen guide
> Be nothing better than a wandering cloud,
> I cannot miss my way.
> —*The Prelude*, Book I, 16–18

More than a program of free wandering, these lines could be a definition of the new liberty: the liberty that guides the steps of the walker and will guide the steps of the Republican armies can be defined as the impossibility of losing one's way, the immediate certainty of the direction indicated by the accumulation of perceptible signs. On that July 14, this liberty can be recognized everywhere by the bunting that decorates the windows and triumphal arches, as well as in the sound of the wind in the leaves of the elm trees that line the straight roads of France; in the villages where joy shines on people's faces, where all night they dance the dances of liberty.

That is how he saw the Revolution: an unexpected spectacle, which he had not come to see. In fact he tells us it's another idol he worshiped then:

> But Nature then was sovereign in my mind.
> —*Prelude*, VI, 333

But that is precisely what he saw on the roads of France: nature, an immediately visible landscape which is at the same time the place where nature as universal principle of life is reflected on itself and becomes identified with the principle of a renewed humanity. What the young man sees, what the poem describes as the walk progresses, is a spontaneous organization of perceptible signs of this nature reflected in humanity, a series of "natural" scenes separated by the play of sun and clouds: the sun, principle of the visible, and the cloud, companion of the wandering walk and guarantee that it will not lose its way; the cloud, which, playing with the sun, cuts the visible into the sayable, the perceptible into the signifying. There is a landscape of liberty that one who has begun his walk under the sign of liberty recognizes in all its obviousness. He experiences nature as a territory of walking, a succession of scenes, those "descriptive sketches" from which the poet writes his book: *sketches* that are both landscapes changing as the place changes, the moment, and the light; unfabricated—unfeigned—vignettes of the new liberty and of a book's pages, a book of images in which French liberty or Piedmontese servitude express their forms and colors in every village sketch; a book of life in which can be read immediately the

> Lessons of genuine brotherhood, the plain
> And universal reason of mankind,
> The truths of young and old.
> —*Prelude*, VI, 545

This book of fraternal truth puts an end to the Platonic criticism of writing as well as the opposition between the sensory and the intelligible. It is written simultaneously in the sensory and in the soul as a living discourse: no longer a silent tableau, a dead writing or a lying representation, but an immediate presentation of the true. The book is no longer opposed to living speech. The new opposition is between the book and the book. It contrasts the book of landscape, represented in the very flesh of the perceptible, with the dead books of knowledge and prophecy. In Book V of *The Prelude*, entitled *The Books*, the poet lamented the fact that the mind does not have, to imprint its image, an element closer to its own nature than the book. And he illustrated this with the tale of a bad dream the poet had while dozing off over *Don Quixote*. In the bare landscape of a desert he met an enigmatic Arab who presented him with a stone/book, Euclid's *Elements*, and a shell/book in which the prophecy of imminent destruction could be heard. The dream thus portrayed the abstraction of the book in the abstraction of the place, the scene of a fight against evil, of an ethical vision of the world that no perceptible symbol could mediatize. Going from the prophet and the knight-errant to the walker, one goes to a new regime of truth. This is a living form, a principle of schematization able to change the movements of the sun and clouds into movements of belief. There is no longer any need to be summoned to the desert to know good and evil. It is only a matter of walking and looking. Truth is not in some distance that the voice or the sign could point out, at the risk of betraying them. It is not in some model represented or distorted by the image. On the roads of France, in that summer of 1790, no image imitates any model, no idea can be found to be allegorized. By 1793 or 1794, allegory will become necessary, reason will have to be symbolized, the Supreme Being portrayed. But, in that brief time of grace, July 1790, the nation offers itself to itself. What the poet sees, by the roads, along the Saône, or in the solitude of the mountains, is what makes the presentation of the community possible, to know the self-presence of nature. He takes his place this side of politics, in the sensory synthesis that permits politics to be presented in its self-evidence, in its separation from the visible that is the foundation of the community. For Republican politics is no longer ordered from the point of view of a privileged spectator, for the spectacle of royal majesty. Republican politics is that of the walkers. The community is made of people who, while walking, see the same images rise up. Nature has dethroned the king by suppressing his place, his point-of-view—nature in the double sense that will establish, for the new age, the core of politics in sensory experience: in one single notion, the power that causes being and holds beings together and the place where one goes, without privilege, to walk and look about.

We generally credit Wordsworth with being in the first rank of those who revealed nature to poetry, and brought about its disclosure. What it seems to me he first discovered and introduced under this name is a way of seeing while on the move, of fixing the *sketch* in which nature presents itself to oneself, reveals itself as presentation of self. He introduced an idea of the poem as breathing and vision, a kind of schematization that is also the sensory schematization of the modern community, a way of seeing the signs of liberty or oppression—these signs, or rather these quasi-signs, are caught in the self-presentation of a nature that signifies without meaning to signify; a way also of converting the seen into hope, into sympathy or resolution. More profoundly, the poet/traveler to the country of the Revolution grasps the point of identification between the modern aesthetic revolution and the modern archipolitical utopia.

It is the modern aesthetic revolution on which Kant focuses at the time: the dismissal of the *mimesis* and the abolition of the distance between the *eidos* of the beautiful and the spectacle of the perceptible; the ability of the beautiful to make itself be appreciated without concept; the free play of the faculties that proves, even if it neither can nor must determine any concept, a power of reconciliation between nature and liberty. As to the archipolitical modern utopia, I do not mean plans for an ideal community. Utopia for me is not the place that exists nowhere, but the ability of overlapping between a discursive space and a territorial space; the identification of a perceptual space that one discovers while walking with the *topos* of the community (2). In the identification of modern aesthetic with modern utopia is founded a singular ability for the community to make itself also appreciated, loved without concept, to identify its master signifiers (nature, liberty, community) with the place and act of a poetry conceived as free play of the imagination. The result of this, in Kantian terms, is the transformation of reflective judgment into determining judgment. In the free play of imagination, reason in effect presents itself directly as determining a world. Thus the poet can characterize this time

> When Reason seemed the most to assert her rights
> When most intent on making of herself
> A prime enchantress—to assist the work,
> Which then was going forward in her name!
> —*Prelude*, XI, 113

Reason seems then to be given the perceptible substance of its experience and its verification. It provides dreamers, as well as those carried away by the imagination, the substance with which they can make their evidence and their hope:

> Then doubt is not, and truth is more than truth,—
> A hope it is, and a desire; a creed

Of zeal, by an authority Divine
Sanctioned, of danger, difficulty, or death.
—*Prelude*, IX, 404–7

The enthusiasm provoked by this sensory coming into being of reason is the aesthetic-political principle of what, at the very time of farewells to great hope, the preface of the *Lyrical Ballads* will proclaim as the principle of the new poetics: the communication of *feelings* and of natural associations of ideas in a state of *excitement* (3). A principle of the politics of the sensory: against the hierarchies of representation, poetics is identified with a general aesthetic that expresses the laws of feeling, the conveyance of sensation in general. This poetics of sensation, after the farewell to the revolution, will apply itself to recognizing in the life of ordinary people the purity of this play of sensations, and in their language the medium of their intensified expression. But it is first of all the utopian production of the *we* of the community which gave a face to this sensory community that authorizes the stroll of the "I" toward the daffodils, and identifies this movement of discovery with the writing of the poem conceived as communication of the movement of sensation. This identification between writing and communication is developed in the original experience when

> . . . I remember well
> That in life's every-day appearances
> I seemed about this time to gain clear sight
> Of a new world—a world, too, that was fit
> To be transmitted, and to other eyes
> Made visible.
> —*Prelude*, XIII, 367–72

From one transport to the other, it is not only the great revelation of the new world that is content with the discovery and glorification of simple people and simple things. Lyric subjectivity and its horizon of community are established only at the price of a critical effort that separates the "wandering" of the poetic "I" from the poetic utopia of politics. The newness of the aesthetic community is also that of a dividing line that is maintained, always fit for transgression, between the universality of the aesthetic community and the archipolitical objectification of the link. This is a dividing line always to be redrawn, and it is undoubtedly that which explains why, fifty years later, the old poet, friend of order and religion, sets out to rewrite his "descriptive sketches" of an enthusiastic walker in the country of the Revolution, not to change their appreciation, but to complete their communication. Poetry asserts itself as the ability of a sensory community to grasp anyone and anything in poetic *wandering*, by going back over the route of the inaugural walk, by dissociating the rhythm of its walk from that of citizen armies, the clouds of a summer sky from political storms. The poet accomplishes this in an extraordinary way in an "apolitical" poem that speaks to the operator of political-poetic transport: "To the Clouds." Where are you going? he asks the brilliant army of clouds. Question without answer. Nature no longer displays the power of the community, it no longer works on behalf of politics. This is not only because the Revolution is over and the poet has come back from it. It is not enough to put an end to the Revolution. One must put an end to it with writing, make the cloud that accompanies poetic utterance solitary, separate it from the course of the army of clouds that swing on the horizon, as all glory and empires do. In this separation the path of lyrical enunciation is won:

> . . . a humble walk
> Here is my body doomed to tread, this path,
> A little hoary line and faintly traced,
> Work, shall we call it, of the shepherd's foot
> Or of his flock?—joint vestige of them both.
>     —"To the Clouds," 53–57

The humble path, the line that goes from the "I" to the "daffodils," which makes the "I" glide in harmony from simple words to simple things, is also the line of demarcation between the poetic approach and the political march. Lyric writing, uprooted from representative heteronomy by its identification with the sensory writing of politics, must separate itself from it to recover its autonomy. The path of lyrical utterance is that of a re-writing. That is why it is not very important to dwell solemnly on the reasons for Wordsworth's precocious failure of creativity, or on his tendency towards repetition. The poet does not repeat himself out of lack of creativity. He devotes himself to rewriting as if to his task. Lyric writing is a rewriting that is traced starting from a necessarily lost writing:

> As through a book, an old romance, or tale
> Of Fairy, or some dream of actions wrought
> Behind the summer clouds.
>     —*Prelude*, IX, 300 ff.

THE DOUBLE JOURNEY

Can re-writing avoid being a disavowal? Not just a political disavowal, but a forgetful denial of the very status of the poem? Can the writing of a poem settle quietly down into being the simple gesture of a liberty that lets it go from a simple feeling to simple words to speak to simple people about simple things? Isn't it in this single movement that the poet forgets what writing means and what liberty signifies? That is the question encountered by the next generation of poets. It's not just that these poets bitterly feel Wordsworth's and Coleridge's betrayal, Jacobins reconciled to the social order and to the contemplation of their lakes—and castigated for it in the buoyant verses of Byron's *Don Juan*. The younger poets also denounce the carelessness of this writing assured of its power and its words and above all that word of all words, the password *liberté—liberty*, a borrowed word that the natural acceptations of the native word "freedom" will never be enough to ensure. There is no simple feeling and no simple word. Liberty can't disguise itself as the modest figures of the wandering walker or the dazzled freshness of his gaze. It can't pretend to be nothing but the happy spectacle of nature on holiday. Canto I of *Don Juan* jibes at tired heroes in this ironic lesson in literary morality:

> The regularity of my design
> Forbids all wandering as the worst of sinning.
> —*Don Juan*, I, VII, 51–52

Byron, for his part, will not deny himself any digression. But his digressions will more than once have as their object of ridicule the way the former Jacobin Wordsworth yesterday "season'd his pedlar poems with democracy" (*DJ*, III, XCIII, 4), and today "with what complacency he creeps,/ With his dear '*Waggoners*' around his lakes." (*DJ*, III, XCVIII, 875–76.)

To refuse the enchantments of *wandering* is to mark the distance between words and things, the same distance that is exacerbated in the fate of the word *liberty*: a word devalued by the Reign of Terror in the French Revolution and the imperial war; a word made even more opaque by the ambiguous insurrections in Spain and Portugal. The sonorous words of French liberty have been perverted into acts of oppression. The wars of liberation in Spain and Portugal have been turned against the very ideas of liberty and emancipation, in the shadow of religion and monarchy. Nowhere do the words of liberty coincide with its deeds; its voice cannot be found in its proper place. Thus the politics of the poem cannot be a simple policy of accompaniment. It passes by the movements that seek to give liberty its own language, to make its voice coincide with its place. Thus the wandering course of the knight Harold, leaving the England of lakes for the ocean of the poem, takes a well-defined direction. He will go first to the place where liberty makes itself heard without knowing itself (the Iberian peninsula) and from there will head toward the place which is its native land, even if its voice can no longer make itself heard there (Greece). But that also means that the parody of the medieval *romance* becomes by the same token a simulacrum of the epic journey, the journey of a hero who, traveling again to the places of the effaced revolution, makes the lyric land of clouds, lakes and daffodils return to the native country of the epic. At this price, it is possible to give back a place to the voice of liberty and a voice to its place. The indecisive subject who in medieval garb completes the journey from modern England to ancient Greece introduces a crack in lyric simplicity. Modern lyricism, just recently emancipated from the constraints of genres, must invent a new sort of epic. Already in Wordsworth the snapshots of the dazzled walker were accompanied by the long, fourteen book, eight-thousand-line story of the "growth of a poet's mind." But *Childe Harold* pays witness to much more than this: the newly emancipated lyric poem must go and refound its liberty by means of a return voyage to the land of master signifiers. The lyric "I" must uphold its autonomy by reintroducing, even if it means annulling, the feeble support of a fictional hero/antihero. A unique fiction, since it is nothing but the thread of the journey that leads these debased words back to their source. By returning to the epic, lyric affirmation reinvents it. It invents a new meaning for it. It identifies it with the fiction of a return journey: return to the origin of meaning, to the place where metaphoric transport is reinsured against the usury and betrayal of words, where liberty is recognized as the living principle of every relation, of every deed that gathers words and things. Through these phantoms or mockeries of epic that are called *Childe Harold* or *Don Juan*, the epic takes on a retrospective face that will dominate modern thinking about poetics. It is identified with the return voyage. The Odyssey becomes the very metaphor for the poetic transfer [*transport*] of meaning, for its wandering liberty and its original roots. Lyric speech asserts itself by coupling the ghost of an epic with an equivocal status: an initial identification of the written page with the traveled space, along with a denunciation of the trickery of the lyric "I." This duplicity is perceptible in the dual way Childe Harold travels the distance from Spain to Greece: first according to the rhythm of the journey, but second by way of a gap in the poem, as in this singular appearance of the Greek Parnassus right in the middle of a description of a chorus of proud Andalusians:

> Oh, thou Parnassus! whom I now survey,
> Not in the phrensy of a dreamer's eye,
> Not in the fabled landscape of a lay,
> But soaring snow-clad through thy native sky [ . . . ]
>
> Oft have I dream'd of Thee! whose glorious name
> Who knows not, knows not man's divinest lore.
>     —Byron, *Childe Harold's Pilgrimage*, Canto I,
>     LX–LXI, 611 ff.

Parnassus is the name that is the object of the highest science, that *lore* that the new century would link, for better or worse, only with the name of the people. But it is also, arising in the place where it is being invoked, the "actual" Parnassus that denies the hill of chimerical dream or poetic fable.

Of course there is a simple explanation for this displaced appearance. The poet is in Greece as he is writing down his memories of Spain, and, from the window of the room where he writes, he contemplates, between two Andalusian-colored stanzas, the actual Parnassus. But this simple explanation ignores this: it is the very act of writing that is denied here, the distancing of writing and of fiction. Literature must deny itself to earn the cost of its journey, uttered at the time of departure:

> Words which are things, hopes which will not deceive.
>     —*Childe Harold*, III, CXIV, 1061

The "actual" Parnassus that rises up in the midst of the Andalusian chorus like its truth, the place that gives it meaning, is the immediate identification of a snowy summit and a name that is a master signifier, a signifier of the power of words in general. It is the identity of a word with its native land, of liberty with itself. This identity of the name and of the thing is not produced by Greece. Nor does Greece produce free men. Yet it still contains their identity for whoever knows how to capture its shadow. And it is this shadow that the wild freedom of the Andalusian virgins lacks. There is no more magnificent chorus in Greece. Only the shadow that gives meaning is lacking from its splendor. They only lack:

> . . . such peaceful shades
> As Greece can still bestow, though glory fly her glades.
> —*CH*, I, LXIV, 655–66

The double journey of the poem gives the Andalusian chorus twice the Greek shadow it lacks. In vain does Byronic irony make fun of the ingenuousness of travels around a lake; his voyage from the modern Ocean to the ancient Mediterranean also is furnished with all the guarantees of not losing his way. This path is already traced. The freedom toward which the poem travels has already traveled the path from the opposite direction, from east to west, according to the great teleology that the era had sanctioned and that is deployed in the "Ode to Liberty" that the Spanish insurrection inspired in Shelley. The history of freedom is written as a series of stanzas carried by the movement of waves whence arises, at the onset of a stanza that prolongs the movement of one single sentence, some fortress of cloud or stone, as in the leap from the fourth to the fifth stanza:

> . . . when o'er the Aegean main
>
> Athens arose, the city such as vision
> Builds from the purple crags and silver towers
> Of battlemented cloud, as in derision
> Of kingliest masonry: the ocean floors
> Pave it; the evening sky pavilions it . . .
> —Shelley, "Ode to Liberty," 60–65

The story of freedom can be written as a succession of stanzas in which each stanza represents, come from the wave or alive in its trembling, a rest, freedom moving forward, falling back. This freedom continues to exist in reflections, echoes, flowers already unfurling under the surface of the water. It writes its story in regular, rhythmic stanzas, in voices and in echoes. The history of the world is structured as a poem. Freedom is itself the first lyric-epic speaker. It writes a stanza here, another there, and persists in its very disappearance: reflection of light on the surface of the water or transparency of the image in the deep. The poem that comes after makes it move from place to place and resound, echoing itself. It gives its voice as a pledge of its place, its past as a pledge of its return:

> Within the surface of Time's fleeting river
> Its wrinkled image lies, as then it lay
> Immovably unquiet, and for ever
> It trembles, but it cannot pass away!
> —"Ode to Liberty," 76–79

It is true that this assurance is soon contradicted by the voice of the narrator. At the end of the poem, when the song is about to fall silent, the waves close back on the voice that they had allowed to go by. Of course a poem must bring itself to an end. But in *Childe Harold*, it is initially the tension of a double relationship between words and things that is marked: from the enthusiasm of the traveler en route to a country "where words are things" to the radicalism of the skeptic who proclaims "Away with words," knowing that words have no effect other than seduction. The "new epic" that returns to the primal land of the truth of words also reopens the distance between the subject/poet and the subject of the poem. The journey toward the native land must be entrusted to a fictitious character, but also a false character. "I am looking for a hero," proclaims the first line of the first canto of *Don Juan*. But the era, widowed already of any muse that could be invoked, no longer offers heroes to sing of. Not because it lacks them—on the contrary it creates them and sends them back to nothingness every day in its newspapers. One single character, then, will present himself for the journey, the only modern character to have worthily confronted the descent to Hell, *Don Juan*, the liar, the seducer. The epic that follows the traces of Ulysses the liar can only have as its hero an antihero, Don Juan, Childe Harold, or Eugene Onegin. The character that fascinates Byron's, Pushkin's, and Leopardi's generation, the seducer, is the man who knows that words are only words, only means for capture, who identifies freedom with the indefinite potential of drawing advantage from their radical vanity. The dream of the word that is like things has as its exact counterpart, with these three poets who conclude the revolutionary age in poetry, the nihilist discourse of the seducer who speaks the nothingness of words and the undefined freedom of the one who utters them, even if it means denying himself, if necessary, as a seducer. At the extreme is the figure of Eugene Onegin, the seducer who no longer uses words of seduction, and who scorns the words in the love letter of Tatiana, who offers herself to him. This parody of epic, where the romantic politics of the poem is achieved, locates lyric utterance in the undefined balance between the truth and lie of liberty.

## The Captive Swallows

It is precisely this balance of freedom between truth and lie to which Mandelstam devotes his poem "The Twilight of Liberty" a century later, in May 1918. Here it is not a question for him of deploring the loss of political freedom. First of all his twilight, like Baudelaire's, can belong to the morning as well as to the evening. And the logic of the images and the meaning seems to point to morning. But it is not the dawn—glorious or parodic—of the new age that he sings of. What is at issue in this uncertain twilight is precisely liberty's centenarian tie with its metaphors, with the forms of transport that, for a century, have escorted it, have made it travel from evening to morning or from morning to evening, from east to west or from west to east. Mandelstam means to show this: liberty has neither a fixed course nor a territory. It does not authorize any subject of utterance to drift along with it, within and without, all along its wording, with the same step as that of solitary walkers and fighting armies. The poem does not prolong or repeat any journey, even a conflicted one, of words with things. The journey has no other place but in the poem. The poem cannot be the breath of nature or History. In Mandelstam's poems, the air is frequently called, with reason, unbreathable, as dense as earth or as suffocating as water. And the cause of this impossibility of breath is clearly indicated by the poet: the air "trembles with comparisons," the earth "rumbles with metaphors" (from Osip Mandelstam's "Finder of a Horseshoe"), just as the image of Athens floated on the waves of Shelley's poem. The elements are saturated by these images that draw to them words that have gone in search of things, and it is this saturation that "The Twilight of Liberty" makes us feel:

I

Let us glorify, brothers, the twilight of liberty
The great twilight year.
In the frothing nocturnal waters
Is plunged the heavy forest of traps.
You rise over dark years, O sun, judge, People!

2

Let us glorify the burden of fate
That weeping the leader of the people carries
Let us glorify the shadowy burden of power,
Its intolerable yoke.
Whoever has a heart must hear, O time
How your boat sinks to the bottom.

3

Into warring legions
We have chained the swallows. And look:
The sun is invisible; the entire element
Whispers, trembles, lives.
Through the nets—thick twilight—
The sun is invisible and the land floats away.

4

Well, let's try, then: an enormous, clumsy turn
A grinding turn of the wheel.
The land floats away. Men, act like men!
Like a plow, dividing the Ocean,
We will remember until the cold of Lethe,
The ten skies our land was worth.
   —Osip Mandelstam, "The Twilight of Liberty"

The twilight of liberty is this first of all: the word *liberty* is immersed in
the thickness of twilight. The twilight, in fact, is neither the beginning nor
the end of the day. It is day that is like night, day in which one cannot see
the sun. This "sun, judge, people" is however said to rise, but precisely "on
dark years." The revolutionary sun, the sun that transforms at will into a
judge and a people, is an invisible star, not illuminating, caught in the hazy
tissue of its resemblances, of its indefinite metaphorization. The thick haze
that surrounds the sun, this opaque fog chirping with chained swallows, is
the haze of all words and all images that, for a century, have not ceased es-
corting it, or that it has not stopped accompanying. The thick twilight of
liberty is the plenum of Romantic nature, the master signifier of the nineteenth century that, from vignette to vignette and from journey to journey,
has filled all the cracks between the intelligible world and the perceptible
world. This poem echoes Mandelstam's polemic prose pieces against the

nineteenth century, the bulimic century, starving for actual or metaphoric journeys to travel the earth or sound the sky or the sea; the invertebrate century, octopus with a thousand arms, greedy to grasp everything in all directions; the century of eaters of words and devourers of spaces, which has drawn the thick veil of its words-like-things and its spaces saturated with writing between the fragile enunciating subject and his sun—this sun that illumines the subject only at the price of keeping things at a distance and reminding him by each of its sunsets of all the time that has mounted up for him. The nineteenth century, according to Mandelstam, has not stopped protecting itself against this threat. It claims to be the century of History, but it is rather the anti-historical century, the "Buddhist" century (4). The "progress" it has invented is the refusal of historicity and of death that supports its meaning. This phantom of history is only the summary of its journeys in all directions to fill in, with the mucilage from its tentacles, all the empty spaces of meaning, time, and death. The invisible or blind sun that rises on the years of revolution is the misty sun bogged down by its tentacles of an omnivorous century.

The revolutionary twilight first of all signifies this: the sun that rises like the light of the new proletarian age is the dark sun of the age of writing that eats spaces, greedy to cling to its things and their places. Its warring legions are made of chained swallows, of words bogged down, stuck to the tentacles of the octopus-century. Mandelstam goes back to the problematic point of coincidence between the evidence of poetic accompaniment and the perceptible evidence of politics. But he refuses the comfort that consists in turning away from sensory political synthesis. On the contrary, one must think about this synthesis poetically, to inscribe into the poem the point of coincidence of politics and poetics. One must construct the space of this coincidence poetically, reveal it by constructing it. For the space of coincidence always presents itself as already there. Freedom always guides our steps to it: or shall we say it precedes them, it has always effected poetic-political synthesis in advance, the synthesis of the visible and of its meaning. To escape the power of synthesis, one must invent a place of writing that places the political signifier *liberty* in the poetic signifier *twilight* to reveal and dissipate its shadows. Mandelstam's politics is, more strictly than with anyone else, a politics of the poem. And it matters little to inquire whether the poet approves of or condemns the Soviet revolution, if one must take seriously or treat as parody those songs of glory that celebrate the power taken on in tears by the leader of the Bolsheviks just as previously, the popular choruses of Mussorgsky paid tribute to the glory of *Boris Godunov* who was also begged to accept the burden of the crown. The same goes for the reference made six years later to

> The wonderful promise to the Fourth Estate
> An oath profound enough for tears.
>    —Mandelstam, "January 1, 1924"

In truth, the song of glory to the usurping tsar was already a song of shared suffering. Similarly, definite suffering and possible derision are included in the song of glory to the revolution. Its thick mist can equally open up to a new light or darken into an irremediable night. And the poet's responsibility is involved in it on his own territory, the use of words. It is up to him to make the Soviet cloud seen in the light of the poem—the "sun of Alexander," or the one whom all Russia calls Alexander Sergeivitch: Pushkin (5)—or else to bury there that sun of writing, or make it into the torch or flashlight of militiamen, of "Pushkinists with great-coats and revolvers," the artists of the "little Soviet sonatina" who will make the keys of the Underwood rattle in chain reactions, the doorbells at early morning and the rattle of chains ("Leningrad"). For the "wonderful promise" to be kept, freedom must be liberated from the "heavy forest of traps." The proletarian army of liberation is itself a forest of traps in the night, because this night is already a forest of traps, it is peopled with words similar to things and things similar to words: *soleil/peuple* [sun/people] or the cruiser *Aurora* [dawn], forest of traps, forest of symbols left in the middle of the night of liberation as well as every night by the tentacles of the Romantic century.

In fact we must recognize the critique of symbolism in all its breadth, a critique that, for Mandelstam, aims not just at the circle of Russian Symbolists alone, but at an entire practice and philosophy of language that are indissolubly a philosophy of History and a practice of politics. And for that, we must have a thorough understanding of what a symbol is. A symbol is not necessarily an enigmatic image that at once shows and hides some more or less profound meaning. More fundamentally, a symbol is a word or an image—a representation—that can function only in a relationship of resemblance with an Other. That is the heart of Mandelstam's politics against symbolism, expressed notably in the essay "On the Nature of the Word": symbolists have neither words nor things, only the ghosts of words and the ghosts of things, only images that resemble other images: "The rose is the image of the sun and the sun the image of the rose; the turtledove is the image of the young woman and the young woman the image of the turtledove. Like animals to be stuffed, images are emptied of their substance and filled with a foreign substance. In place of a 'forest of symbols,' we have a taxidermy workshop full of stuffed animals [ . . . ]. Formidable contradance of 'correspondences' that exchange signs of complicity [ . . . ]. The rose indicates a young woman, the young woman the rose. Nothing wants to be itself" (6).

To the "Buddhist" philosophy of History corresponds this use of images that at once empties words of their materiality and things of their utensility and their "habitability." For there to be a world and History, there must be words and things constituted in mutual distance: words weighing with all their materiality, constituted in themselves like so many citadels, "little Acropolises"; there must be things that satisfy both material hunger and spiritual hunger; there must be a risky flight of swallow-words that wheel freely around things, choosing as a lodging-place a signifier, a substance, a body (7). On the other hand, symbolist practice seals images in resemblance, dematerializing with one movement every word and every thing: "On all words, on all images, they have affixed a seal, reserving them for an exclusive liturgical use [ . . . ]. At table, there is no question of eating: it is not a real table [ . . . ]. With the utensils, it's revolt. The broom invites us to the Sabbath, the pot refuses to cook, demanding for itself an absolute meaning" (8).

The symbolist capture of the poem and the state capture of the revolution go together. The sun of the revolution has risen in this symbolist space of resemblances. It is "judge" and "people" in revolutionary prose or song in the same way that it is rose in the poem or that the young woman is a turtledove. As long as the revolution is not liberated, it recruits its armies from captive swallows, it lives the fixed images of symbolist practice. The revolutionary State—like any State but following an even more imperious necessity—feeds on warring legions that are birds, makers of Spring, on warships that are the *Aurora*, on sunrises that are the dawn of new times, on plows that dig for harvests of the future or on ships that launch into the sky. The State in general needs words and the new State particularly needs to cling to the images of new life. Hence its summons to the imagination of creative artists. The State needs culture because it needs to give itself flesh, form, color, a sex. In its way, it feels what the poet asserts: the need to live historically. Only, to live historically, one must have words and things that are free with regard to each other. Of that the revolutionary State wants to know nothing. It does not have the time. It conceives of History in the manner of the century it has inherited, the Buddhist century: as a protection against time and death. It needs words and images quickly to give itself a body, to make itself perceptible and to protect itself. The State calls for and devours the words and images of culture and art to protect itself against devouring time. This appetite for "culture" forms an accomplice to the "anti-philological rage" where symbolist practice ends. It makes it the devouring ogre of words. And the poet's task is indissolubly to protect the State against the consequences of its devouring fever:

"For the life of the word, a heroic era has begun. The word is flesh and bread. It shares the fate of bread and flesh: suffering. The people are starving. The State is starving even more. But there is something even more starving: time, Time wants to devour the State" (9).

Sought out by the State to give it these words of which he is the warder, the poet will assert his heroic and eucharistic calling by devoting the word to the face of the monster who wants to devour the State and make it devouring: Time.

"Whoever raises up the word and offers it to time, as the priest does the Eucharist, will be a new Joshua. There is nothing hungrier than the contemporary State, and a starving State is more terrifying than a starving man. Compassion for the State that denies the word, that is the contemporary poet's social function and feat of arms" (10).

We can evoke Walter Benjamin here, who also evoked Joshua when discussing the anecdote where the fighters of July 1830 are supposed to have shot at clocks to stop monarchic time. Mandelstam, like Benjamin, wants to stop "time that passes," the time of conquerors and of their "inheritances." But the comparison stops there. The act of stopping the sun—a certain sun, that of the Buddhist century—does not refer in Mandelstam to any Messianism, any valorization of the time of epiphany. The nineteenth century for him was not too "historicist," it was not enough so. It did not know what historicity means: the constitution of a framework of free words and free things that gives a skeleton to the century, that "unites vertebrae." That is how the fight against the State that devours words is also a sort of compassion toward it. That is the "glorification" unique to the poem, the part it bears of the burden that the blind guide of the people carries by night. The poet diverts the function of provider of words that the revolutionary State concedes to him for the sake of serving the culture. He diverts it so as to raise the word to the height of time and thus to give the revolution the framework of a new century, a historical world of things and words taken from the circle of devourings.

To present the word to the face of time is to work in two directions of time, doubly revoking the simple journey of the lyric *I* toward its flowers and the simple epic return toward the earth of master signifiers. It is, on one hand, a work on the present. One must win from time that passes and from the misty space of resemblances the event of the free and hazardous meeting of words and things, that "instant of recognition" that is possible only through separation, through the science of the farewell. The problem is not exactly to give a purer meaning to the words of the tribe—the swallow of spring, the sun of the new world, the cock of the rising sun, the ship of the future or the plow of future harvests. The problem is to *unseal* them, to give their sonorous substance the possibility of wandering freely in order to make itself the soul of every body, to be the lamp that serves as a shelter for the flame of signification, or the word-flame whose sonorous substance shines in the lamp of signification. In the Soviet night—the night of resemblances—the blessed word, the "raving" word, must be made to shine, the word that evades the interminable game of complicities to give the "joy of recognition" to the "seeing fingers" of someone still in fog. Thus it is possible to tear the poetic signifiers of the new life from their state-symbolist appropriation, to give them back their power: the power that the Russian language maintains from its double origin, from the Byzantine marriage of Hellenic culture, and from the Christian Word: from the word made flesh of Christian religion and from the legend of Psyche, the soul, visitor of the Underworld, as Apuleus' tale places her at the heart of late Hellenism—a power that has passed into the very heart of the Russian language, to which it has transmitted "the secret of the Hellenistic conception of the world, the secret of a free incarnation, *thanks to which the Russian language has become flesh animated with sounds, flesh gifted with speech*" (11). It is this active flesh of the word that must be risked in the Soviet night to provoke the event, the lightning of the encounter. The suffering of the Christian Word is identical to the free joy of Greek Psyche. The heroic calling of the poem is one with its ludic calling. The politics of the poem is the identity of them both, which hunts equally the phantoms of art for art's sake, or of art at the service of the proletariat:

> In Petersburg we will meet again
> As if we had set the sun in earth there,

And the blessed word, the raving word
We will utter it for the first time.
In the black velvet of the Soviet night
In the velvet of the universal void,
Still sing the dear eyes of the blessed ones
Still blossom the everlasting flowers.
  —"In Petersburg"

But the immortelle flowers only at the risk of a voice forever ready to lose itself: word forgotten on lips, swallow fallen in the snow, disembodied idea that returns to the sojourn of shadows. It is only in the night unique to the poem—the night of separation—that the signifiers of freedom can be liberated. By taking the title of his *Tristia* from Ovid, Mandelstam takes over the matrix image of the night of separation. But separation is no longer the unhappy accident of which the poet sings in his lines. It is the very principle of the poem, the science of the poet. "There is no happy space," Rilke writes, "that is not born from separation." For Mandelstam, there is no poetic power except from the point of view of exile. There is no moment of recognition except by the power of separation that divides "the frothing nocturnal waters," which is not a farewell to the Soviet night but the interior movement that rearranges it and makes visible the stratifications of meaning and image that compose it:

I have learned the science of farewell
In disheveled lamentations in the night [ . . . ]
Who can, saying this word, goodbye,
Know what separation it brings to us
What the cock's crow foretells for us
When the flame burns on the Acropolis
And at the dawn of some new life
When on his straw the bull chews slowly,
Why does the cock singing the new life
On the walls of the city beat its wings?
  —"Tristia," 1–2, 10–17

The flame of the Acropolis, the ox of the Christmas crib, the rooster of the rising sun and of betrayal form the Hellenic-Christian device of visibility that transforms the Soviet night and the signifying framework that the century must fashion for itself to be able to think of its historicity. Thus the other aspect of the poetic labor on time takes on meaning: the return of the chernozem [the fertile black soil of Southern Russia and the Ukraine—

Trans.] of time, which puts at the poet's disposal all languages, the arrangements of words and the signifying sedimentations of the past. "Classicism,"
writes Mandelstam in "On the Nature of the Word," "is the poetry of the
revolution." And he calls again for Homers and Pushkins, Ovids and Catul-
luses. But the clearly anti-futurist provocation of this call in no way makes
the culture of the past an encyclopedia placed at the disposal of the young
revolution. For Ovid and Catullus, Homer and Pushkin, in one sense, have
not yet existed. Their words and lines are still unfulfilled promises, instruments whose major possibilities are still to be discovered. Thus we must tear
them away from the continuity of time—from the little Soviet sonatina—
to replay them on the "flute with a thousand holes," give them a new power
of event. But it is not a question of return to the native land. There is no pilgrimage to the native land whence the new harvests can be blessed. There is
only the plow turning over the same soil to make the layers of time emerge
from it:

> Well, let's try, then! An enormous, clumsy turn
> A grinding turn of the wheel.

This ship's wheel of time soon becomes the "plow dividing the ocean."
Metamorphosis of elements on the scale of the twilight confusion where revolutionary freedom has its place. Perhaps this vessel/plow symbolizes most
closely the criticism of Romantic metaphoricity: metaphors for the native
land of master-signifiers and the waves that make them travel from century
to century or give passage to the Odyssey of return; metaphors for journeys
to underworld sojourns by which the historical continuity of meaning is assured. Mandelstam poetically closes the era of organized journeys to Parnassus or Lethe, which gave a voice to the place or a place to the voice. He closes
the era of happy journeys to the country of the dead or to native lands. There
is no longer a journey of words in the poem that can be at the same time the
metaphorical journey toward the place of the first significance. Greece is no
longer the land beyond the poem that implicitly or explicitly guarantees poetic *wandering* [English in original]. It is wholly within the poem, in the place
of writing that it constitutes. The best image to define this place is the one
that Mandelstam uses for Dante, that of the polyhedron. Mandelstam's
Greece is entirely within the polyhedron that the poem shapes and polishes
in the opacity of the spoken word of the world in general, and of the spoken
word of the new life in particular. It has burst forth in many facets there, re-

flected many times in the play of transparencies that it produces. One cannot go back, in the course of the poem, from the Petersburgian present of the revolution to the Greek dawn that might give it its original meaning. Greece is inside Petersburg/Petropolis, Peter's city of stone [*la ville de pierre et de Pierre*] that the poem builds in the place of writing:

> Goddess of the sea, terrible Athena
> Take off your majestic helmet of stone
> In transparent Petropolis we shall die
> Where you do not reign—Persephone does.
> —"We Shall Die in Transparent Petropolis"

The poem that makes the Neva and Lethe transparent to each other teaches us this in one fell swoop: there is no beyond-place that is both in the poem and outside of it. Lethe, the river of the Underworld where the passage of meaning ventures, could not be the useful river of Romantic transfers, the river that the historian Michelet boasted of having crossed so many times to give a voice to the deceased, and to nourish present generations with the sap of the land and of the dead. The transparency of Lethe is that of the wave that separates, that organizes the encounter of souls and bodies only in their separation. It is not Athena, the goddess of the philosophic owl, the protector of all fortunate odysseys, who governs the relationship of the Neva with Lethe, but Persephone, the goddess of death. We must take the measure of this change. All of modernity had until then placed itself beneath the shadow of a Greece of return. It constituted the identity of the epic with the thought of the complete journey and of the glad return. It made the epic an encyclopedia, in the strict sense: circular and exhaustive journey of words through places. It made Ulysses the traitor, the liar, the hero of a certain truth, one that travels round the world and encloses it in the words of a book. That is what Mandelstam slices into. As to epics, he knows only books of division: the *Iliad*, or the second book of the *Aeneid*, which tells of Troy's last night. He knows that no one ever returns home, not even Ulysses, about whom the modern age has obstinately forgotten that he was condemned to wander until he found the country of men who do not know the sea. No one returns to Ithaca or to Athens as to his native land, to the natural abode of words and things in harmony. Every Athens is a destroyed Troy. In the polyhedron of the poem, the forest of snares of the Petersburgian night or the forest of symbols bequeathed by the Buddhist century, the primordial scene of division and treason is repeated: the forest of Achaean lances in the stomach of the wooden horse attacking the city of stone.

All of Greece is originally divided by this poem, the foundation of the Hellenic. And this division is also a tension in Mandelstam's poetic thinking. For there is in him a final Hellenic dream, insistent in its programmatic prose. With the architectural and technological dream of futurism he contrasts the dream of a Greece of the hearth, a universe of essential objects made sacred by the "little acropolises" of the Russian language. Thus the text "On the Nature of the Word" evokes this domestic Hellenism granted to the literal Hellenism of the Russian language: "This Hellenism is the milk pitcher, the *oukhvat*, a piece of pottery, a household utensil, crockery, in sum a whole physical environment; Hellenism is also the heat of the hearth felt as something sacred, it is any possession, any element of the outer world that's connected with man, any clothing you put on your shoulders with a sacred shiver [ . . . ] it is humanizing the surrounding world and heating it up to the subtle heat of a teleology. Hellenism is a stove next to which man sits and whose heat he values as if it emanated from himself" (12). But the ensuing lines transform this beautiful abode inhabited by the mind into an Egyptian ship of the dead: "Finally, Hellenism is the funerary barque of the Egyptians in which is placed everything necessary for the dead man to continue his pilgrimage on earth [ . . . ]." As for the poem, its discipline leaves no place for this pleasant Hellenism of the hearth. It is only in prose that the program for a new domestic Greece is expressed, celebrated by the liturgical function of poetry. The poem discovers the stone chamber of domestic immortality as already occupied by the wood of the Achaean arrows, horse, and ships. The "high abode" of Priam is a "forest of ships"—a vertiginous metonymy that sets up the flight of the Achaean ships—the "long flight of wild cranes" of the famous Catalogue of ships in the heart of the Trojan city. The Achaeans have destroyed, in advance, the dream of a Hellenism of objects. The flame of the hearth or of the Acropolis is identical with the fire of the Trojan night. Greece's origin is the place of an irremediable betrayal:

> Because I did not know how to keep your hands in mine
> Because I betrayed your tender, salty lips,
> I must wait for the dawn in the drowsy Acropolis.
> —"Because I did not know," 1–3

Biographers have busied themselves with "finding" here the name and history of the woman thus abandoned. But she has no other identity than the one that is given her by the very poem that constructs the place of betrayal:

> The Achaeans in darkness prepare the horse [ . . . ]
> Why did I leave you before the time had come,
> Before the night paled and the cock crowed,
> Before the burning axe planted itself in the wood?
> —"Because I did not know," 5, 10–12

And the name itself is given in another "love poem" of the Petersburgian night, which tells of not having sought to appropriate betrayed lips:

> I sought in the flowery instants
> Cassandra, neither your lips, Cassandra, nor your eyes.
> —"To Cassandra"

The name "Cassandra," the name that is lost in the "dry rumor of blood," is the Trojan name par excellence: the girl of the high palaces destroyed by the Achaean wood, the foreigner with a swallow's speech who, in Aeschylus' *Agamemnon*, dies while announcing the sinister day come from the Trojan night and the net of treason held out for the leader of the Achaean fleet. But she is also the young woman who, in *Tristia*, the eponymous poem of the book, bends over wax to tell the future and die of it:

> And it is thus: the transparent figure
> Lies on the immaculate slab of clay
> Like the stretched skin of a squirrel.
> Leaning over the wax, the young woman observes.
> It's not for us to probe the Greek Erebus
> Wax is for women what bronze is for men
> Only in combat do we meet our fate.
> But women die telling the future.
> —"Tristia"

Note the singularity of this figure behind the transparency of the poem. The sexual distribution of tasks seems modeled on the twin figures of Greek vases: warriors with spears and shields outstretched, women priestesses of the domestic cult. But the sexual division of work and the community of fate in death are constructed as a trompe-l'oeil. Even though Cassandra and

Agamemnon in Aeschylus die together, in fact they form a pair: aggressor and victim—for one, victory in the peril of homecoming, for the other the always vain knowledge of defeat. And we, too, know the price of this vain knowledge. The other, the young woman, Cassandra is gifted with a power of seeing as well as its implacable counterpart: the impossibility of being understood. But this fate is the penalty of a very particular act of defiance. In legend, Cassandra is punished for having refused herself to Apollo, the god of the Muses. Thus she represents the dissociation in the heart of poetic promise, in the heart of any politics of this promise. And it is the very act of the poem that makes this dissociation operate, to deny its own utopia:

> In the black velvet of the Soviet night,
> In the velvet of the universal void
> Still sing the dear eyes of the blessed ones.
>      —"In Petersburg"

The happy figure of singing eyes must be contradicted: eyes that see do not sing. The one who looks at the wax is not heard in the night of arrows. The act of the poem is carried out in the trajectory between vision that cannot express itself and the joy of recognition offered to the "fingers that see" [in "I have forgotten the word . . . "]. But the hazardous trajectory of swallow-words is not just at the risk of the oblivion that makes the bird swoop down on the snow. It is at the risk of betrayal, of a primal connection with the warring arrows in the Trojan night. The risk of betrayal, then, takes precedence, for the *I* of poetic utterance, over any question of political disavowal. The question is: at what price is one assured of not losing one's way? Can one both *see* and *be understood*, stretch the revealing surface of the poem and take part in the concert of the new life? Apollo is perhaps not exactly the new "god of journalists" made fun of by Hölderlin. But he could well be the god of all the cockcrows, all the manifestoes and avant-garde movements that provide the revolution with its poetry—those manifestoes in which the drunkenness of the Acmeist flute with a thousand holes competes with the drunkenness of the hundred-and-fifty-thousand futurist words. We have already observed that it is in the prose of the builders that the optimism of the new poetic church is always defined in Mandelstam. But the poetics of the poem is not that of manifestoes. The score of the poem holds Apollo and Cassandra together, the dear eyes of fortunate ones and the song of the new life. The happy trajectory of the swallow-words, of Psyche-words hellenizing the objects of the hearth turns out to be at the cost of the betrayal of those unheard lips. And the night of separation ends also in a dilemma: the poem sends this question back to the poet: doesn't he have to choose between being the thrower of word-arrows or the unheard seer? The Eucharist of the manifesto that the poet offered the poem becomes the passion to which the poem forces him. Nothing can appease the dry rumor of blood. The program was to give the century its skeleton. But it is blood alone, mixed with quicklime, that can weld together the vertebrae of the century. And the poet must with the same force assert that he is and is not a contemporary of the time of "Muscovite confections," in any case not as a priest raising up the Eucharist of the Word. The score of the poem, deployed to produce the happy instant of recognition, tends to withdraw toward the figure of the impossible, the pure outline of lips forever betrayed:

> The memory of the Stygian bell
> Burns on my lips like black frost
> —"I have forgotten the word"

> Human lips,
> when they have nothing more to say
> Keep the shape of the last word spoken
> —"Finder of a Horseshoe"

> Remember my words forever for their taste of sorrow and smoke.
> —"Remember my words . . . "

Mandelstam leads the *I* of poetic utterance to the point where it can no longer accompany anything, where it becomes the rumor of blood and burning on lips. He chose to stop being an "understood" poet even before being sent to his death as a maker of epigrams all too well understood by the artists of the "little Soviet sonatina," the "Pushkinists with revolvers and great-coats." The epigram on the "mountain dweller from the Kremlin" is dated 1934. But eleven years before this suicide-poem, Mandelstam had written his poem-testament, "Finder of a Horseshoe." The horseshoe figured as the last metonym of Pindaric ode to the glory of Olympic victories, relic of poetic language glorified by the name that it glorifies, but destined hereafter to be a door ornament or archeological remnant:

What I say now, it is not I who say it,
It was dug up like grains of petrified wheat [ . . . ]
Time clips me like a coin
And already I miss a part of myself.
          —"Finder of a Horseshoe"

These days it sometimes happens—and I am thinking particularly of the declarations of someone like Czeslaw Milosz—that people contrast the poetry of the East, poetry of flesh and blood, which has been able to preserve the lyric tradition and the epic humanitarian breath in its struggles, with the sophistications of a Western poetry exhausted by the imperatives of formalism and Mallarméan hermeticism. Mandelstam's experience shows the artifice of such a division. The "formalism" of Mallarméan restrained action nonetheless preserved, even in the act of throwing the dice, the conquering gesture and communion with the crowd, silent guardian of mystery (13). The avant-gardist decision allowed the poet to absent himself from the political scene in order to "prepare the celebrations of the future." Keeping the relationship between the future and the past blank, it sketched a possible alliance of poetic and political avant-garde movements. Conversely, the extenuation of the lyric *I* and the entry into silence to which Mandelstam is led arise from his very confrontation with the great lyric and epic tradition. Because he has stirred the "compost of time" to set in the poem the master signifiers of the poetic-political game, because he has thought rigorously, in the time of the greatest political rigor, about the politics of the poem, Mandelstam has the experience of the loss of the lyric *I* in an irremediable separation:

Age of clay! O dying century
I fear that only he will understand you
Who lives inside the abandoned smile
Of someone lost to himself.
          —"January 1, 1924"

# TWO

# Rimbaud: Voices and Bodies

Let us start with three well-known formulations of Rimbaud's. The first summarizes a program: "I prided myself on inventing a poetic language accessible, one day or another, to all the senses" ("Alchemy of the Word"). The second apparently utters its conclusion, resolved or otherwise: "For sale: bodies, voices, immense unquestionable opulence, what will never be sold" ("Sale"). Between the two, the third insinuates its question:

> What is meant by my words?
> It makes them run away and fly.
> —"O saisons, ô châteaux"

What can we understand, then, in Rimbaud's speech, how can we define this "genius" that determines its flight? How should we think of the impression of sense of his poem between a project—the new language, the word accessible to all the senses—and its liquidation—I won't say its failure, since the sellers aren't at the end of their sale, and the salesman doesn't have to give up his commission?

There are two great ways of not thinking about this flight. The first, the biographical method, identifies it with the running away of an individual about whom we know that he used to be precisely a runaway child. The second uses a freeze-frame: the runaway is also a seer. "Seer" means visionary or prophet, a figure of the past century who was still honored during the Surrealists' time but is scarcely appreciated today. But it also means a lover of images, an illuminator, maker of those *painted plates* [English in original] that are, according to Verlaine, the *Illuminations*. The interpreter can then let the prophet play out and pause to consider the design traced on the "painted plate." Of each illumination, he will seek the translation, the one the poet has "reserved," who also said: "I alone have the key to this wild parade."

Whoever looks for the key to a text ordinarily finds a body. Finding a body beneath letters, inside of letters, was called *exegesis* when Christian scholars recognized in the stories of the Old Testament so many *figures* of the body to come as the Incarnation of the Word. In our secular age, it is commonly called demystification, or simply reading.

## The Body of the Poem

At the end of 1961 a journal called *Bizarre* published, under the initials R. F., a text entitled, "A-t-on LU Rimbaud?" [Have we READ Rimbaud?]. In it, the author, Robert Faurisson, *read* the sonnet "Les Voyelles" [The Vowels], that is to say he named the body that the seemingly random play of vowels outlined, for one unconcerned with the words. If the red of the I claimed to be "beautiful lips," and the omega the "violet ray of *her* eyes," one could identify the meaning of the poem with the body of the woman to whom "her eyes" belonged. And that, of course, had been said in the title, if one knew how to read it: VOYELLES, or VOIS-ELLE [See her]. In order to see *her*, you just have to turn the A upside-down, so that it obviously represented the female sex; to turn the E on its side to admire the proud eminences of two snowy breasts; again to turn the I on its side to outline beautiful lips; to turn the U upside-down to give it the undulation of a head of hair. Thus we reach the O, supreme trumpet, and the violet omega of her eyes, and we understand the glorious effort of some *He* procuring for the body lying among the letters that intense sensation of seventh heaven expressed in the violet ray of her eyes. By dint of this one saw "Elle" [She] in "Voyelles," and could display to the prudery of literature professors and to the verbosity of philosophers what it really is to "read" a poem. In short one confirmed both the detective story adage (*Cherchez la femme*) and Hippias' saying, the adage of demystifiers: Beauty is a beautiful woman. A beautiful poem is the representation of a beautiful female body.

Literature professors and scholars of Rimbaud reacted uneasily, with mixed emotions. All in all, though, one is always happy that there is a body in a poem, even if it is not precisely the one that decency requires. And this disappearance of the body of the letter within the presentation of its "seen" meaning answers quite well to what we often understand by the term "reading." Have we read Rimbaud? Have we found in him the L of reading [*lecture*], the L of the wings [*ailes*] of inspiration and the ELLE of the fulfilled completed feminine body? The L-Elle in which the reader gazes indefinitely at his reading reflected?

But Rimbaud does something else. He does not *read* the poems of Rimbaud. He writes them. And in particular, he has already, in advance, written his "reader's" interpretation. And he has already had it decided by the woman involved. The woman in question is not that *Venus* by Bouguereau whose tempting forms Faurisson displays to support his demonstration. She is a certain Nina to whom the poet has already suggested, in vivid lines, that she stretch herself out so that he can speak to her, tongue to tongue:

> Eyes half-closed . . .
> I would carry you, trembling,
> Onto the path:
> [ . . . ]
> I would talk into your mouth;
> I would walk, squeezing
> Your body, like a child I'm putting to bed,
> Drunk with blood
>
> Which runs blue under your white skin
> With rosy tones:
> And speaking to you the frank tongue . . .
> Look!—you know already . . .
> —"Les Réparties de Nina" [Nina's Rejoinders]

The problem is exactly that Nina does not know this tongue. To this language-to-come of language, she replies with this famous rejoinder: *And my office?* The office is the workplace that the serious employee recalls to her dreaming lover. But it is also the place of accounts [*écritures*] that sends the poet back to his writing. "Nina's rejoinder" is more than a facetious remark. It is what presides over a first division of the poem, what prevents it from being written as the other side of its reading, what prevents bodies and lines from lying together at the behest of the voice. Two things, in fact, are missing from this operation: language and woman. "Today when they are so lit-

tle in agreement with us," Rimbaud writes elsewhere. We must take this declaration of disharmony or "non-agreement" seriously. Undoubtedly it is inscribed in a configuration from the time: the one the Saint-Simonians determined by marking the empty place of the woman in the couple/humanity of
the future: the empty place of one who cannot yet be classified, who has not
yet known and declared herself. But what is not yet said, and what thus prevents the *speaking* of the new humanity from entering the order of a new *doing*, can be written in the form of the poem. And Rimbaud gladly writes it in
an essential image: precisely the image of the eyes or the feminine pupils that,
far from any blissful expression of satisfied desire, on the contrary mark un-
certainty about its nature. With that I'll return to "Soeurs de charité" [Sisters
of charity], a poem that suspends an identification (woman/sister of charity)
that was one of the *topoi* of the poetry of the century:

> But, O Woman, mound of entrails, sweet pity
> You are never the sister of charity, never
> [ . . . ]
> Unawakened blind woman with immense pupils,
> All our embracing is just a question.

The pupils' immensity belongs to the unawakened blind woman. Between the unspeakable pile of entrails and the image of the sister of charity,
the eyes of *Her* are precisely a blind point: point of blinding, of illegibility
that separates the body of the poem from the body of its "subject." The unawakened blind woman is the true "enigma" of the poem, the look that is
missing from the harmonious agreement of the text and the vision.

The poem represents this enigma as an image. But it also hammers it out
in the regularity of alliterations that stretch over its entire breadth the music
of the L's and R's of *l'aveugle irréveillée* [unawakened blind woman] and her
*prunelles* [pupils]. For giving the color of the vowels does not go without the
complementary action defined in "Alchimie du verbe" [Alchemy of the
word]: "to fix the form and movement of the consonants." And the line that
fixes the color of the vowels (*A noir, E blanc, I rouge, U vert, O bleu, voyelles*
[black A, white E, red I, green U, blue O, vowels]) has at least two other
particularities. First, it is a perfect hexameter, a Latin verse, then, rather than
a French verse. Secondly, right at the start it makes the conflict of the L's and
R's ring out, which will give the poem its perceptible body, a body of writing perhaps more consistent than any reproduction of a Bouguereau:

"co*r*sets ve*l*us, g*l*aciers fie*r*s, f*r*issons d'ombe*ll*es, *r*i*r*e des *l*èv*r*es be*ll*es et
vib*r*ements divins des me*r*s vi*r*ides" [hairy corsets, proud glaciers, shivers of
umbels, laughter of beautiful lips and divine vibrations of virile seas] that
lead the music of the sonnet to the paroxysm of the "sup*r*ême c*l*ai*r*on" [fi-
nal trumpet].

Assuredly the play of liquids and their combinations is essential to any
poem as it is to the common fare of language. But Rimbaud carries it to its
extreme; he makes it an obsessive music that takes on the fluidity of every *L-
elle* in the jaw of the R's: ostinato of trumpet and drum that consumes the
Rimbaldian poem line after line, from the rhyme of the "t*r*ois *r*ou*l*ements de
tambou*r* (th*r*ee d*r*um *r*o*ll*s)," the "g*r*and so*l*eil d'amour cha*r*gé (g*r*eat sun
with love bu*r*dened)" and the "b*r*onze des mit*r*ailleuses (b*r*onze of machine
guns)" to the prose of "nous massac*r*e*r*ons les *r*évo*l*tes *l*ogiques (we wi*ll* massac*r*e *l*ogica*l* revo*l*ts)" and "fanfa*r*e at*r*oce où je ne t*r*ébuche pas (at*r*ocious
fanfa*r*e whe*r*e I do not falte*r*)." Music of the initial of his name, the R of
Rimbaud indefinitely pounded with trumpet and drum beats. It is also a music that is quite certain of the mother poetic tongue, Virgil's Latin, that of
*Arma virumque cano,* of *Tu Marcellus eris,* or of *Insonuere cavae gemitumque
dedere cavernae.* Music of childhood at which the little Rimbaud was already,
at the age of fourteen, hammering away, in the first of the Latin poems that
remain to us by him, "Le Songe de l'écolier" [The schoolboy's daydream]:

Ver erat et morbo Romae languebat inerti Orbilius

Let us pause a moment on what, for us at least, is Rimbaud's first line. At
least two characteristics are remarkable in it. First, it is the fanfare, if not the
cacophony, of the r's. Then there's the brutality of the introduction of the
subject *Ver erat.* "It was spring." No doubt the good student Rimbaud was
could have found in his *Gradus ad Parnassum* the method of introducing it
with a few bird-twitterings, with water streaming or trees budding. In place
of this he brutally imposes the dull sound of the three letters *Ver* that serves
as homonym in a dizzying way for poetic spring, the verse [*vers*] of the
poem, the color green [*vert*], and the worm [*ver*] that is in fruit, the worm
of evil of which "Alchemy of the Word" will tell us that it is nothing other
than the worm of "happiness."

This first word of the poet Rimbaud might move us less if it didn't happen to be also the first word of a poem whose subject is the enthronement
of the poet. For that is the daydream of the little Orbilius: in the midst of

swans and doves, Apollo himself appears to him, come on a cloud of gold. And the god will write on the child's forehead with a celestial flame these words, in capital letters: TU VATES ERIS: you will be a poet, formula of enthronement in which every Latinist will hear an echo of Virgil's *Tu Marcellus eris*, the promise of greatness made by the poem to the imperial inheritor whom death has already seized, the invocation of the great promise to the dead child on whom the next part of the poem, just as famous, pours handfuls of lilies (*manibus date lilia plenis*). We will find these handfuls of lilies again in the next poem, "L'ange et l'enfant" [The angel and child]: in it, the child is called to heaven by the angel. But the little dead one, having become an infant of heaven (*coeli alumnum*), will appear with his angel's wings to his mother, will smile from heaven at her who smiled at him (*Subridet subridenti*), and will, at the last line, come to join his divine lips with his mother's lips:

*Illaque divinis connectit labra labellis*

This *labra labellis*, "lips to lips"—to which Nina's lover will have no right—is precisely what the "laughter of beautiful lips" [*rire des lèvres belles*] of "Voyelles" phonetically translates: translation of the letter of one poem not into her "body" but into the letter of another poem. The adjective *belles* that qualifies these lips gives them no quality. What it does is literally transcribe the Latin of *labellis*. And their laughter does not signify the pleasure of any lady. It refers to the mother of the dead child, of the child who writes as dead in a dead language to join his lips with those of his mother. This translation of the Latin into the French does not give us the "sense" of "Voyelles." And it is not a matter here of explaining "Voyelles" but of determining the voice that allows the poem to be articulated, the voice that generates itself from a kiss of dead lips, from a "successful" communication of lips to lips: communication of the dead child, of the dead poet, with the mother, who makes the severe counterpart of Nina's *rejoinder*, refusing the invitation of one who wants to make a language of his tongue to lay her down on the path of poetry.

The "beautiful woman" of Hippias and Faurisson, the beautiful woman of the demystifier, thus turns out to be neatly cut in two, even if—especially if—the division is represented as one single image, the image of the enigma: the immense pupils of the unawakened woman. The body of the poem, its unrepresentable body, is this din of language around a gaze about which we do not know what it sees or what desire it signifies: din of a language of childhood that is also a dead language around a secret that it [*elle*], that an ELLE [she] will never tell us.

We can say a little more about this ELLE by reading "Après le déluge" [After the flood]. Here we understand that she is not the amiable Eucharis, the one who says it is spring. In fact it's something of an open secret that it's spring. The poet knows it from the first word of his first poem: *Ver erat*. The holder of the secret is not the pleasant muse who scatters the treasures of the poem's Noah's Ark, the "peace of the sown pastures of animals." It is the other one, the one who gives the alchemist wrinkles: "the Queen, the Sorceress who lights her embers in the clay pot" and "will never want to tell us what she knows and what we do not know."

Of course, it is tempting to call this queen by the name of the one who has her lips kissed by the dead child, the one who for her pain and for the pain of her children bears the proper name whose initial is insistent in the roll of the alexandrine drum: in other words, the mother, Madame Rimbaud. Around this sorceress queen, the poem can certainly be unified in its very dispersion, starting from the enigma of a glance, the "blue look that lies" of the "Poètes de sept ans" [Seven-year-old poets]. Starting there, "Voyelles" can be seen as the coat of arms of the poem itself. We would find:

—in the letter I, the origin and destination of the poem: those "beautiful lips" that are surrounded by spit blood, anger, drunkenness and repentance;

—in the letter U, the Word's alchemical program that claims to exist both in the drunken boat's descent toward the open sea (the divine vibrations of virile seas) and in the labor of a studious saint or old man (peace of wrinkles/ That alchemy imprints on great studious foreheads);

—in the letter E, the poles of its journey: framing the primitive scene— the "shiver of umbels" trampled by the "too upright" mother of "Mémoire," the white of the high polar ice, the white of the Magi kings and the tents of Africa;

—in the letter A and in the black corset of flies buzzing around cruel stenches, the obsessive image of the other source of the poem: confronted with the enigma of the look and with the contact of cold lips, black symbolic insect of an obscure object of desire, mixing the smell of latrines with that of summer and the scent of the skin of the working girl across the way: "the drunken midge in the inn's pissoir, in love with borage," the "dirty flies" to which the field is handed over, as well as to forgetfulness, by the "Chanson de la plus haute tour" [Song of the highest tower].

So we're not so much able to give a key to the poem as outline its body of utterance, the sensory network over which the first disagreement of look and lips is distributed into themes and registers where bodies and voices join and separate. "Voyelles" could give us the body of utterance of the Rimbaldian poem: the configuration of the signifiers of the family novel in the shape of a poem machine.

By determining the poem's body of utterance, we encounter a distinct interpretation of Rimbaud's writing as an inscription of the family romance. I am thinking here of Pierre Michon's fine book, *Rimbaud le fils* [Rimbaud the son]. Commenting on the matrix-like role of the Latin verses, Pierre Michon sees in them "funny little gifts," "bits of hackneyed phrases" that the son offers to the mother's desire and in which the mother, without even knowing Latin, can recognize a chasm even more profound than her own, so profound in fact that the son ends up swallowing up his mother in it. The consequence is that it is strictly speaking the buried mother who writes the Rimbaud-poems: the mother knocking in the "dark closet" her son has locked her in; the sorceress who does not say what she knows but knocks strongly enough to break the language of the poem in the son's lines, to break that "great twelve-foot curtain rod" of the alexandrine on which the family novel was hung.

We could describe things that way. And Pierre Michon does so with gusto, raising *bio-graphy* to the height of its concept: life-writing, life written, life in writing, the equivalence of one to the other. But the consequence is risky—there might not be too much to do with the detail of the poems. In fact it would be enough to note the mother's kicks that put its music in motion. The products of these kicks lose their importance, and even more, the poetic art or politics that they can express. If it is the mother who writes in the son's closet, the poem itself is perhaps condemned to the status of a fragment, a scrap or object of little piles, little "scraps of black air" [*bouts d'air noir*] as the "Fêtes de la Faim" [Feasts of hunger] say: air as song and as atmosphere, but also as the homonym for the initial of Rimbaud's name [the French letter "R" is pronounced "air"—Trans.]. Since one scrap of air or black R is as good as another, we can then let the actual gesture of the poem fall into insignificance.

## The Legend of the Century

That is one solution: to identify the mechanism that produces the kicks and turn the construction of this identity not into a commentary on the poetry of Rimbaud, but into another poem. That seems a reasonable option, and the poem worth making. But isn't that reasoning a little too fatalistic? From the fact that men do not make "their" history, as first Rimbaud and then we had thought, should we conclude that they, and Rimbaud first of all, do not even make their poems, that they never do anything but transcribe the blows of the mother buried within them? Here we will take another side. We will postulate that Rimbaud himself says something that deserves to be thought of intrinsically, that an occurrence of a unique thought carries Rimbaud's poetry beyond the transcription of the family novel. This event couples the family novel and its childhood Latin with another legend and another music, the great music of the nineteenth century: science on the march and the new work on which dawn is breaking; superstition conquered, new love, the woman who will reveal herself and the light in the East; the future city and its glorious bodies, the brotherly choirs of new work and new love.

This coupling occurs with a blare of trumpets, with an experiment, and a utopia of language: the invention of a poetry that is already, in advance, the language of future harmonies; a theory of voices and bodies, a practice both anticipated and anticipating the concord to come. It is this invention that the "Lettre du Voyant" [The letter of the seer (letter to Paul Demeny, May 15, 1871—Trans.)] plans, and that the movement of "Le Bateau ivre" [The drunken boat] mimics. Of course we no longer read these texts with the eyes of the Surrealists. While they read of the freedom of the future, we ourselves feel the refrain of the time, the *topoi* of nineteenth-century prophecy. That is perhaps because that century has completed its long path in our own. But that is also because a few, Rimbaud first of all, set it down in writing for us; because Rimbaud included all the dimensions and all the cardinal directions of his century in the layout of the poem, because he wrote down its code.

To think about this "writing" of the century in Rimbaud has nothing to do with the classic search for influences. Vain disputes continue forever on that subject. Some argue that he must have read *this or that* (Fourier, Enfantin or Eliphas Lévi for instance) at the Charleville library or at the place of his friend Bretagne who cultivated occultism. Others look in vain for these works in the catalogues of the time in the library and ask where he would have found the time to read all these social theories and occult sciences whose trace they want to find in his poems. But once again, it is not a question of reading, but of writing. Rimbaud does not read the theories of his century; he writes down the century that unites them. And, whatever those who think themselves erudite might say, to write down a century does not require so many preparatory studies—simply an attentive look that comes across some series of writings that ordinarily are never encountered on the same shelves. To write the nineteenth century, one must for example come upon:

—some of Flammarion's lectures and one or two volumes by Figuier;

—a few numbers of the *Magasin Pittoresque* and of the *Tour du Monde*;

—some vaudevilles by Scribe and some opera librettos by same or by one of his colleagues;

—one or two accounts of World's Fairs;

—a handful of those pamphlets that were published by the bushel by the disciples and sub-disciples of Saint-Simon, Fourier, Ballanche, Azaïs, Wronski and by all the inventors of the new religions of love, society and labor—pamphlets in which are inextricably mixed regenerated language, cities of the future, the emancipation of women, the promotion of fertilizer, the development of byroads, workers' housing, future androgyny, efficient stoves and eternity by the stars.

To this corpus it is enough to apply a few suitable models of reading: some primers, prayer books, songs or fairy tales. With that, an *attentive* mind can put the century into the layout of the poem. That absolutely does not mean to summarize its theories or sing of its hopes. It means to trace the line that joins its signifiers and its scattered emblems, for instance:

—woman and the railroad;

—the Crystal Palace and working-class music;

—the dance pavilion and the Orient;

—*Michel et Christine* and the flood of barbarians;

—*La Dame aux camélias* and the new Christianity.

We can find all these links, chosen from among many others, within Rimbaud's poems, or rather we can find that they *are* the poems. We could then go beyond the interpretative disputes that classically set two camps against one another, camps I will call respectively the Identifiers and the Fantasifiers. The former set out to recognize the places and scenes described by the poems. For instance they localize the Splendide-Hôtel from "Après le déluge"—some place it across from the Paris Opéra, others in Scarborough or elsewhere. The latter retort that Rimbaud never went to Scarborough and that in any case there is nothing to see on the *painted plates* except the free play of poetic fantasy. Eventually, a third group will come to reconcile reality and fantasy by testifying that these are visions, hallucinations, of which opium and hashish are the only causes.

It seems obvious that none of these three attitudes fully accounts for what the Rimbaud fragments present to us. Let's take, for instance, the series of "Villes" [Cities] in the *Illuminations*. It offers us a journey through the century, arranged in the space of a vision whose levels are confused and disjointed. In the city of the fragment there are many cities or fragments of "cities of the century": the industrial metropolis, the New Babylon girded with its suburbs; the Charles Fourier city of the future with its galleries and passageways; the phantasmagoria of World's Fairs and Crystal Palaces; the bandstands and the esplanade of Luna Parks, the city that puts on spectacles of the entire universe, that raises up in its theaters, its festivals, and its stage sets of forests, mountains, waterfalls, deserts, the Orient, the Pole. But there is also the city already written as phantasmagoric by the visionary poets and the opium-smokers, the city of Baudelaire, of Poe and of Thomas de Quincey.

For Rimbaud's "hallucinations" have singular properties. Even while admitting that some are the effect of hashish and that the "method" of "Matinée d'ivresse" [Morning of drunkenness] is that of the "poison" that upsets the senses to make their new language appear, these "actual" hallucinations are strangely faithful to the Baudelairean description of the effects of the drug, and to his adaptation of Thomas de Quincey. The landscapes in *Illuminations* more than once recall those in [Baudelaire's] *Paradis artificiels* [Artificial paradises], those dream cities with their "proud buildings spread out like stage sets," their "museums that are packed with beautiful forms and intoxicating colors," their "libraries where works of science and the dreams of the Muse are stored," their "concerted instruments that speak with one single voice" and that are like the gift made to the visionary—and to him alone—by "the work and martyrdom of all humanity." And some lines from the fourth chapter of *Paradis artificiels* could summarize the way in which the alchemy of the word and the transformation of the city are gathered together in one single vision: "Jagged landscapes, fugitive horizons, perspectives of towns whitened by the corpse-like lividity of storm or illumined by the gathered ardours of the sunset; abysses of space, allegorical of the abyss of time; the dance, the gesture or the speech of the actors, should you be in a theater; the first-come phrase if your eyes fall on a book; in a word, all things; the universality of beings stands up before you with a new glory unsuspected until then. The grammar, the dry grammar itself, becomes something like a book of 'barbarous names of evocation.' The words rise up again, clothed with flesh and bone; the noun, in its solid majesty; the adjective's transparent robe which clothes and colours it with a shining web; and the verb, archangel of motion which sets swinging the phrase." [Charles Baudelaire, "The Poem of Hashish," from *Artificial Paradises*, translated by Aleister Crowley.]

Thus the city of the hashish-eater or the opium-fiend is already written, already identified with a space of pilgrimage between city and suburb, which is the space, too, of a singular encounter, the one related in [Rimbaud's] "Ouvriers" [Workers]: the walk taken one warm February day by two "betrothed orphans," the poet and his "dear image," his wife in the cotton skirt of the last century and in the bonnet with ribbons. Granted, this Henrika in the checked skirt could be Verlaine, as some would like, or a free creation of the poet's fantasy, as others prefer. But in the end Baudelaire has already made these betrothed orphans of the New Babylon and its suburbs enter the legend of the century under the names of Thomas de Quincey and his prostituted and yet chaste Anne, the same Anne who is also the sister in the fairytales, the one who looks out of the highest tower, from which she descends in "Feasts of Hunger" to flee on her donkey into a countryside of stones.

Here again, it is not a question of a biographical key. It is a question of a code of the century. That is one of the encounters that encode the century: the encounter of the two orphans on the streets of the New Babylon. An orphan boy: the family son who escapes the rules of his tutors, he is the passerby, the poet, the experimenter of the future. An orphan girl: the daughter of the people, the virgin and prostituted woman, who in Rimbaud will be identified with the city itself: the virgin and martyred city, prostituted by the past, the bearer of the future, the "whore Paris" of Parisian orgy, that is to say of the Bloody Week that keeps in (its) clear eyes:

> A little of the goodness of the savage spring.
> —"Parisian Orgy"

Rimbaud does not describe any urban landscape, does not recount any social theory. He does something else: he writes his century. He fixes its codes and its symbols. He checks its coordinates and establishes between them all possible liaisons within the same space. He makes it obvious and, in the same instant, illegible. But he does this while still meaning to do something different. He wants, in fact, to outstrip the century. He aims to give it what it lacks to complete the project of the new glorious body, a language: the language of the future, that of the complete body, of the community of gathered energies ("Voices reconstituted; the brotherly awakening of all choral and orchestral energies and their instantaneous application").

To invent a new language for the new body of the community seems first of all the task of an inventor. But it also the task of a seer, a son of God, linked to what "Angoisse" calls the "progressive restoration of the original freedom," a restitution that, in the Greek of the Fathers of the Church, is called *apocatastasis*: the restoration in its integrity of the body that existed before the Fall.

In short, the coupling of the family novel with the song of the century and its new language, of individual salvation and collective salvation, requires very precise conditions. Rimbaud soon perceived that it signified two things in one. The new language virtually has two names: one, which poses no problems, is alchemy; the other, infinitely more formidable, is the New Christianity.

Alchemy of the word: the thing can be conceived easily enough. It is a question of making the word into gold: placing the words of the century in the light of a directly illuminating sun, once the veil of "the azure that is dark" is torn off. Pictorial plan of sparkling light in the heart of things, in the Impressionist manner, a philosophical plan of a neo-pagan humanism, placing light in the heart of things to make it shine in human relationships. Behind this project that will cover the close of Rimbaud's century and the beginning of our own, we recognize the classic paraphernalia that the inventors of the century keep forging anew with the materials inherited from the preceding century: a little Cabala, a little secret wisdom of the ancient hieroglyphs, a little general grammar and primitive roots of languages, combining the virtues of universal language with the powers of the language of mysteries.

But Rimbaud knows that the new language requires a little more than the alchemical mess: something at once vaster and more restricted. He knows,

UNIVERSITY OF WINCHESTER
LIBRARY

he tells us that he is—whether he wants to be or not—in the West. And he soberly localizes this West: "this land here, and Christianity." Despite all the Illuminist and neo-pagan hardware that we can rattle and that half a century is getting ready to rattle, Rimbaud knows that the new time has only one real name, the one that Saint-Simon gave it: the New Christianity; that is to say not a new effusion of brotherly hearts, but, much more radically, a new resurrection of the body.

## The Hell of Salvation

The question of religion in Rimbaud is one that we do not approach without displeasure. It fatally evokes the polemics on the poet's "conversion" and the maneuvers of that infernal trio Isabelle Rimbaud–Paterne Berrichon–Paul Claudel. Whatever opinion one may have about it, the fact remains that, as he tells us himself, "theology is serious." The question of conversion is a point of biography or hagiography that interests only the clericals and the anti-clericals. But the question of the New Christianity is indeed the heart of *Une Saison en enfer* [A season in Hell], that is to say, the work in which the project of the alchemized word and the changed life is asserted and sold off. Theology is serious. The inventory of the new language of the glorified body knows that "to speak the new language" is described, in the New Testament, as "speaking in tongues" and that it is a charisma: a miraculous power of "walking on water" evoked in "Nuit de l'enfer" [Night in Hell]; a gift and an apostle's power that presuppose charity, but that presuppose it by placing it at an infinite distance from what is commonly meant by that term. Charity is the absolute gift of one who has received everything. He must have, as "Night in Hell" asserts again, a "wonderful heart": not the expansion of a good heart, but the gift that only the Resurrected One can provide (1).

But there is only one Resurrected One. We can always replay the Sermons on the Mount, the Passions, Last Suppers, missions of the apostles and speeches to the Athenians. And the nineteenth century did so unremittingly, once the Saint-Simonians arranged its dramaturgy. But we do not replay the Resurrection. We'll say it in another way: we do not escape a salvation that has already occurred, one that, having already occurred, is the true hell: the new hell, that of parody. Rimbaud, of course, like the Saint-

Simonian apostles, would prefer to escape this constraint. He reassures himself with optimistic declarations: "That was truly the old hell. The one to which the Son of Man opened the gates." Unfortunately, it's nothing of the sort. Rimbaud knows this: the new hell is "the recitation of the catechism." And one cannot escape it with the derisory argument that it's a case of mistaken identity, and that one has never been a Christian. "Night in Hell" does not lend itself to the convenient excuse of "bad blood." The "true poison" is the tyranny of baptism, the obligation of salvation, without which charity is ineffective, without which it is exhausted in more or less scandalous or grotesque parodies of kissing lepers and of redemptive love: pathetic parodies of "L'Époux infernal" [The infernal husband] in which the Angel of Charity is transformed into the lady of the camellias vainly devoted to adoring her "cruel idiot."

So the song of the future glorious body is gnawed in advance by the gaping jaw of hell, of a salvation that has already occurred. It is made derisory by the glorious body of the Risen One who commands all charity and all charisma. Theology is serious and Rimbaud is one who takes seriously the religious discourse of the century, who does not put up with some flimsy little bit of new Christianity, or with any comfortable theory of Evil, the kind Joseph de Maistre provided Baudelaire with. Evil is in the salvation that lies before anyone who wants to go ahead of the century. It is not simply nature that "takes place" and to which "one will not add," a Mallarméan axiom that allows one to draw the poem from the nothingness that is unique to it. It is *grace* that has taken place. It is the transfiguration of the perceptible that has taken place. You can call this transfiguration false and a "stealer of energies" as much as you like; it is still what makes false any promise of a new language, any promise of multiplied voices and of a song of the people. It is what ties together the poem, the lie, and language, and places this great knot across any invention of the poetry of the future. It is also what gives Rimbaud's poetry its singular place between Baudelaire and Mallarmé.

We'll say it in an obvious way at the risk of aping the schematic contrasts of literature textbooks. For Baudelaire, evil can give way to flowering, because one is still within the economy of sin. Evil is the fat gliding cloud that reduces dreams of progress to their illusion. But this fat cloud lets the sun pass by, which illumines a peacefully poetic and pagan nature, the nature equal to itself of living pillars and colors, perfumes and sounds that correspond to each other. Original sin can make the poet a liar, it still leaves nature—and that is the essential thing—in its condition of being a book. With Mallarmé, on the other hand, nature takes place without evil or grace being involved. The paper is virgin so that, from the crystal inkstand, an unprecedented act of the pen can come to inscribe a trail of stars, the mark of a purified language, withdrawn from its ordinary imperfection. Apart from the already-there of nature, the poem has no opposite but commerce. As for Rimbaud, he escapes both of these pleasures. For him, the poem is caught without recourse in the evil of language, in the lie that salvation itself places in its heart. In the heart of the act by which the falsity of the blue gaze of the mother could be absolved in the song of the people, he encounters this other lie: the putrid or cursed kiss of Christ the thief of energies who puts an end to every idyll, as to the one in "Michel et Christine," the putrid kiss of first communions that precede all community.

Rimbaud did not, perhaps, die a Christian. But he knew intensely what the terms of Christianity meant and the place they left for the dream of the poem and of the language of the future.

## The Song of Obscure Misfortune

So what I have called the poem's body of utterance becomes more complicated, this body that was outlined beginning with two plays of lips and gazes: the pinched lips of Nina and the lips of the dead child's kiss; the unawakened gaze of the woman and the lying blue look of the mother. Other lips and other eyes should be included: the lips soiled by the putrid kiss of Jesus, a lover who was happier than Nina's, since he could "choke the throat" of his young lover "with disgust"; but also another eye, as of a one-eyed man or Cyclops, the eye "dripping on their cheeks" of the kids the seven-year-old poet likes to meet, these children:

> Who, scrawny, bareheaded, eye dripping on their cheeks
> Hiding thin fingers yellow and black with mud
> Under clothes stinking from the runs, all worn-out,
> Talked with the gentleness of idiots!
> —"Seven-Year-Old Poets"

We know that it is with only these familiars—this anti-family—that the little poet gives himself over to these "revolting pities" that provoke the mother's terror, the child's protestations of tenderness and the exchange of the blue look that lies. Here we can make use of a strong intuition of Yves Bonnefoy's, which perceives the contrast between the lying blue gaze and the eye dripping on the cheek as the matrix of Rimbaud's whole poetics (2). This unrepresentable eye (what is an eye that drips?), only writeable in its opposition to the mother's gaze, is, effectively, the principle of a whole chain of operations in the poem, of signifiers of the family novel set to the work of the poem. These operators make the knot between the childhood Latin and the song of the people, but unmake it at the same time. By denouncing the lie of the blue gaze and the putrid kiss, they deny any conversion of child-hood pain into a popular song. They do not annul the movement of this conversion, but they accompany it, they invade it with another song: an un-expected timbre, an *ostinato* of the left hand, a song of "obscure misfortune."

We can point to this chain of signifiers in the poem ["Seven-Year-Old Poets"] that describes the "acrid hypocrisies" of the child oozing with obedi-ence: summer [*été*], obstinacy [*entêtement*], stupidity [*stupidité*], tongue stuck out [*langue tirée*], latrines, winter [*hiver*], peeling espaliers [*galeux es-paliers*], idiots, revolting pities [*pitiés immondes*], men in smocks [*hommes en blouse*], outlying neighborhoods [*faubourgs*], drum rolls [*roulements de tam-bour*], starry woods [*bois sidéral*], with veil [*voile*] as a last word. What makes this chain hang together is the encounter, beneath the sign of revolting pity, of two subjects. The first is the little poet locked in his latrine: place of re-fusal and meditation; place of the identity of extremes, of pure thought and of abjection; place of challenge, finally, since it is the place where the Hus-band, Christ, pursues the little girl communicant and since, too, the sub-limity of God's pure love turned to the excremental has been, since the Fa-thers of the Desert, an essential *topos* of ascetic and mystical practice and literature.

The second subject is, from the other side of the wall or of the garden hedge, the children whose eye rubs off on their cheek and the one who sym-bolizes their irruption: the "brutal little girl," the daughter of the workers next door who jumps on top of him and whose buttocks he bites, and brings away in compensation for blows he's received "the flavors of her skin to his room."

That is the encounter that will give the score of the poem its own music and timbre: an imbalance of a resonance entirely different from the one Ver-laine exalted: no longer a question of additional or fewer syllables, but the inscription, within the language of the poem, of the foreign timbre of obscure misfortune or even of impure pain, an idea we can take *a contrario* from "Mauvais sang" [Bad blood], which says: "The clock will not be able to strike anything but the hour of pure pain" [*L'horloge ne sera plus arrivée à ne sonner que l'heure de la pure douleur*]. The imbalance, the singular timbre of this chain of obscure misfortune links the obstinacy of the thought to the consideration of what is not represented in the songs of pain or glory, what is not absolved either politically or religiously—the idiotic or revolting pity of this encounter is expressed in one single concept: a beggar childhood ("Vies" [Lives]). And of course pity is mourning for wonderful charity, the proof of its impossibility. But at the same time it traces the broken line of a still unheard poem, between hymn and threnody. The poem, through pity, becomes the unprecedented music of this imbalance—of this beggary—that comes to work on, to tackle, the great hymns and the great prophecies.

For, in one sense, all Rimbaud's poetry can be summed up in the work that unmakes one single poem, his childhood poem (if we dare say it), "Le Forgeron" [The blacksmith]. "The Blacksmith" is the poem of the century, the poem of the people, of the worker, of poverty and of revolution; the poem in the tradition of Hugo with its great pomp and familiar enjambements and turns. It is the poem of the family romance of the people, the song of great hope and great pain summoning the new language that it lacks. Rimbaud's plan, in brief, the plan of the seer, is to rewrite "The Blacksmith" in a new language, to invent the language of its future.

Yet what he actually does is something entirely different. Instead of remaking a Hugo poem in a language of the future, he will unmake, in the music of obscure misfortune, his own poem, the poem by Rimbaud. The unmaking of "The Blacksmith" in *Illuminations* is called simply, as it should be, "Ouvriers" [Workers]: the poem of the warm February morning and of the unseasonable South that raises "memories of absurd paupers" or the "young poverty" of two betrothed orphans. This South also reminds the poem's subject of "the miserable incidents of my childhood, my summertime despairs, the horrible quantity of strength and science that fate has always taken away from me."

This "horrible quantity of strength and science" distanced by fate offers a formulation that is more interesting than the reproaches addressed to too slow a science. The negative relationship toward science stems less from impatience than from distancing, retrenching. The retrenching of the power of science is due to the stubbornness of a thought that wants to include the un-countable, to put into the poem the dripping from an eye onto a cheek, to make heard the impossible voice of mendicant childhood, as "Phrases" [Sentences] invites us to do:

> My comrade, beggar girl, monster child! It's all the same to you, these miserable women and these schemes, and my embarrassments. Attach yourself to me with your impossible voice, your voice's sole flatterer of this vile despair.

This alliance with idiocy, this obstinacy in coupling with the beggar girl with the impossible voice, is clarified in the inventory that opens "Alchimie du verbe" [Alchemy of the word]: idiotic paintings, unfashionable literature, church Latin, fairytales, asinine refrains, naïve rhythms and other things, including, for the convenience of Faurissons present or future, "sub-literate erotica." What is this clutter, if not the paraphernalia used by Rimbaud in his *Derniers Vers* [Last lines], that is to say in those "sorts of romances" that use the form and vocabulary of "idiotic songs" to tell the dark stories of family history and infernal menages, of workers' paradises, the project of the poet who is thief of fire and rediscovered eternity? One must understand the difference between these idiotic songs—songs by an idiot or to an idiot—and the "good song," which says to the poet:

> Recognize this trick
> So merry, so easy:
> It is only waves, only flora,
> And it is your family! [ . . . ]

> The world is vicious;
> As if that surprised you!
> Live and leave to fire
> Obscure misfortune.
> —"Fêtes de la Patience" [Festivals of patience]

There is no question of leaving to the fire this "obscure misfortune" that "Bannières de Mai" ["May Banners," first section of "Festivals of Patience"—Trans.] proposes on the contrary to liberate. No question of drinking to the comedy of hunger, and of satisfying this hunger that places itself under the invocation of Anne and the donkey [*d'Anne et de l'âne*]; hunger for these idiot and equally inedible things that "Feasts of Hunger" enumerates: earth, stones, rocks, pieces of coal, iron; pebbles a pauper breaks, old church stones, gravel, rocks that are children of the deluge: pebbles of Little Thumb [*Petit Poucet* in Perrault's fairytales—Trans.] running away with his sister Ann, scraps of black air, in every sense of the expression: carbonized pieces of [Rimbaud's] name, bits of lost refrains, fragments of an impossible breath of the poem to come, without forgetting the lifeline tossed out to all the future demystifiers of blood pudding [*boudin noir*, which sounds like *bouts d'air noir*, "scraps of black air"—Trans.].

These scraps of black air that the poem takes to calcine on the utopia of the new song in a way represent Rimbaud's *inventions*, in the musical sense of the word: invention of rhythms and harmonies, of erudite folksongs, suitable for melodically measuring the distance between the song of the people—the song of sorrow redeemed—and the idiocy of the refrain or the nursery rhyme: almost scraps of melody—like rhyme schemes—scraps of language that try to imprison the sun, that is to say eternity, to take the triad of sea/eternity/sun [*mer/éternité/soleil*] in its reduced form: air/soul/pebble [*air/âme/caillou*]. That is perhaps the "last wrong note" [*dernier couac*, which also means "death" in French—Trans.] of which *Une Saison en enfer* [A season in Hell] speaks. It is up to the Identifiers to hear it as Verlaine's gunshot. It seems to me more interesting to connect it to the trumpet of the glorious song of the community. Or if one insists on bringing Verlaine into the picture, he should be added in his capacity as poet. The last croak of the Rimbaud trumpet could then be the last note of a certain Verlainism, the poetry of gallant celebrations and wordless romances: close indeed and infinitely far from the idiotic romance of hunger; the poetry of the "so merry, so easy" trick, of air that has become infinitely labile, infinitely liquid, suitable to be the boiling water that runs over the rust to mix it with the water of Kidron [alluding to "Hunger" (*Faim*) in *A Season in Hell*—Trans.].

### The Four Subjects of the Poem

Perhaps we can now draw up the cartography that holds together *Last Lines*, *A Season in Hell*, and *Illuminations*. *A Season in Hell* gives us the hard core of Rimbaud's program, its political theology or its neo-Christology; *Last Lines* presents us with his notebook of inventions or studies, attempts at melodies and methods that suit the song of obscure misfortune: something like the new *Gradus ad Parnassum* and its parody, the Rimbaud chorus [*or-*

*phéon*], in a way, that brings to an end the utopia of the song of the people, which a half-century earlier had been begun by Wilhem's choral society. [Wilhem was the musician who developed the widespread institution of the *orphéon*, or workman's singing society, in nineteenth-century France—Trans.] As for the *Illuminations*, they give us the other part of the program, revealed in the beginning of "Alchemy of the Word": the display of all possible landscapes and all possible dramas, their Noah's Ark or their encyclopedia. These fragments would give us not the visions of hallucinations or fantasy, but encyclopedia articles, descriptive of this inventory of the representable, which forms the counterpart of the inventory of melodies—and of modes of representation. Alongside the new *Gradus ad Parnassum*, the other tool of apprentice poets: the new Chompré, the *Dictionnaire de la fable* set in the age of Perrault and Offenbach: an encyclopedia of fables for the children of the century, but for children who are a little unusual, those children whom the programmatic poem of *Illuminations*, "After the flood," gives us, the poem that uses the Noah's ark of poetics:

> In the great house of windows still streaming the grieving children in mourning looked at the wonderful images.

The encyclopedia is made for these children in mourning: in mourning for what the Sorceress knows and will not say. It is made for mendicant children: the little saint with his impossible voice. The encyclopedia of images is identical with his grief. It is a grief, or rather a sale, of wonderful images. This sale is not a failure. Or more precisely, it is not a question of failure, but of flaw. The encyclopedia's flaw is that of its subject. The childhood that looks at the wonderful images, the childhood that means to take hold of the encyclopedia of the representable, is in fact divided into four subjects, enumerated in the fragment titled precisely "Childhood" [*Enfance*]:

> *I am the saint*, praying on the terrace—like peaceful animals grazing to the sea of Palestine.
> *I am the scholar* in the dark armchair. Branches and rain beat against the library's casement window.
> *I am the pedestrian* on the main road through the stunted woods; the sound from the canal locks muffles my steps. For a long time I see the melancholy gold wash of sunset.
> *I could be the child abandoned* on the pier stretched to the high seas, the little servant lad following the path whose forehead touches the sky.

The subject of the poem could be the inventor, the scholar in his library, the one whose hibernating comfort only increases as the rain beats on the casement: the calm possession of the materials of the encyclopedia and of the key to every wild parade. He is the inventor who was such a fashionable figure in the nineteenth century, the alchemist of new love, of new language, new labor.

This scholar "with somber wrinkles" is, in short, the dream of the abandoned child—of the child who would like to be a little more abandoned than he actually is (I *could* be, I would like very much to be . . . ). The child might be dreaming of being at once the old inventory of all dramas and all spectacles and the child in mourning—truly in mourning, truly orphaned—looking at his "wonderful images": the child who is son of himself, son of the old man of whom he is the father.

Simply put, between the abandoned child and the knowledgeable old man, two characters are interposed. The first is the pedestrian on the main road who, without a library in Babylon, leafs through the other libraries, the imperfect copies of the absent library, the attics and displays of booksellers; who travels through cities and paths to gather dramas and spectacles, to pile into the poem all places, all landscapes and all spectacles that weave the century, and in particular all those that are concentrated in the stone poem of his great cities, the poem illuminated by the summer night of coal. This traveler piles up all these places and mingles them anew with the imagery of the legend of centuries and the characters from the dictionary of fables, placing the floats of the popular town band on the waves of the birth of Venus and making them resound with Roland's horn. So the space of that century is fed upon by the time of his legend, while conversely the advancing parade of metropolitan progress is invaded by polar ice caps or the dance of savages:

> Guilds of giant singers congregate in clothes and banners blazing like the light on mountain tops. On platforms in the midst of chasms Rolands sound their bravery. On footbridges over the abyss and on the roofs of inns the burning of the sky adorns the masts. The collapse of apotheoses meets the fields of the highlands where seraphic centauresses wander among avalanches. Above the highest crests, a sea troubled by the eternal birth of Venus, charged with Orpheonic fleets and with the rumor of pearls and precious conches—the sea darkens sometimes with mortal brilliance. On the slopes harvests of flowers big as our spears and our cups bellow. Processions of Mabs in red dresses, opaline, climb the ravines. Above, feet in the waterfall and the bramble, deer suck at

Diana. The Bacchantes of the suburbs sob and the moon burns and shouts. Venus enters the caves of blacksmiths and hermits. Clusters of belfries sing the ideas of the people. Castles, built of bone, emit unknown music. All legends alter and elk run riot through market towns. The paradise of storms collapses. Savages dance ceaselessly the festival of night. And one hour I went down into the movements of a boulevard in Baghdad, where throngs sang of the joy of new labor, under a thick breeze, circulating without being able to escape the fabulous phantoms of the mountains where we should have met.

—"Cities [*Villes*], I," from *Illuminations*

It would then be the traveler's privilege to grasp in its totality this city-universe that is also a recapitulation of the legend of the centuries, the unity of ancient mythology and the fanfare of the new labor. But the vision is spelled out only as a parade, the key to which is lost:

> What good arms, what fine hour will give me back that region
> from which my slumbers and my least movements come?
> —"Cities, I"

The reversed order of the adjectives [*bons bras, belle heure*] (it would perhaps be more fitting if the arms were fine and the hour were good) already distances the answer to the traveler's question. Might this be the saint who has the answer or the key, the charity key, no doubt? This saint praying on the terrace like peaceful animals grazing down toward the sea in Palestine—we know him well, too well no doubt. In painters' canvases and pious *images d'Épinal* [popular French lithographs of conventional subjects—Trans.], we have often seen this scholar of a country without rain or window casements. His library has been gutted. One or two stretches of wall, if any remain, just enough to line up a shelf of books of Holy Scriptures and one day hang a cardinal's robe. The saint himself is divided: one hand holds a pen and one hand holds a cross. Dressed in hermit's weeds, he holds next to him the red hat with a tassel; at his feet, a peaceful lion with the face of a good dog is playing with it. It is not this Saint Jerome out of an *image d'Épinal* who will give the fine hour. It is not he who will procure once again a salvation that has already occurred. All that he can do is to leave his mark on the vision. This mark of the saint, of the ascetic, the mystic, is inscribed in the form of these oxymorons of mystic thought that gash the vision: embers of satin, infernos raining with flurries of ice, burning moon, crash of icicles against the stars, fires with the rain of a wind of diamonds hurled by the earthly heart eternally burned for us ("Barbare" [Barbarian]), in short all the metaphors and oxymorons for ice equaling fire, for being identical with non-being, elevation like dejection, that all tell of the impossibility of expressing pure love.

The fine hour is not for tomorrow. And there is nothing left to do but go through all the characters again, to return to the child, to the child's fight with dawn that is delegated to each of the other characters and so on up to the end of the pier that has no end, all the way to "the end of the world advancing." The disorder of the vision is not, then, the sign of hallucination or a play of fancy. It is his fragmentation into the revolving stand of his four subjects. No doubt we can call "this revolving stand" genius, this movement that goes in the winter night "from cape to cape, from tumultuous pole to the seaside, from the crowd to the seaside, from gazes to gazes." That is how it is named in the autonomous fragment. But is it the last word of *Illuminations*? We know that the editors, not Rimbaud, arranged this collection. And the choice often made to conclude it with "Génie" is based on the symmetry of its gesture with that of "Adieu," which concludes *A Season in Hell*. But the symmetry is itself equivocal. "Adieu" makes an emphatic point that is in fact ambiguous. The promise of splendid cities and truth possessed in a soul and in a body goes right along with the burial of a "beautiful glory of artist and storyteller." Absolute modernity assumes, between prophecy and renunciation of illusions, an undecidable semblance. "Génie," on the other hand, is absolutely positive. It forever identifies the movement of great hope with the movement unique to poetry. Whatever hypothesis one makes about the order of composition of *Illuminations* and *A Season in Hell*, "Génie" corrects the ambiguity of "Adieu." It identifies the conquest of future abstemious mornings with the continued struggle of poetry and with the effort of purified language.

But that is what Rimbaud, for his part, refused to do. To understand him, we need again to compare Rimbaud's position with Mallarmé's, as the few lines taken from [Mallarmé's] "Crise de vers" [Crisis of verse] summarize it: "Speaking has to do with the reality of things only commercially; in literature, speaking is content with alluding to them, or with extracting from them their qualities which some idea will embody. On this condition, the song soars upward, a joy alleviated."

For Mallarmé, things as well as words are divided according to an essential distinction. There is commercial reality, and there is a quality one can extract from it so that the word can embody some idea, so that the impure words of the tribe [Mallarmé's *les mots de la tribu*—Trans.] can be purified and can come into the poem "to light up with reciprocal reflections like a virtual glint or flame on jewels." At this rate, the poem can be written as the work of a pure act and can sketch out the place of what it still lacks, the crowd that will one day come *to declare itself.* At this rate, the great invention of the end of the nineteenth century and the beginning of the twentieth is possible, the new future that the closing century invents for itself, by burying the new Christianity beneath the *glissandi* of pagan harps and the afternoon of a faun. This new invention of the future is called the avant-garde.

Rimbaud does not belong to the avant-garde. He does not believe that one can extract the qualities of things and purify the words of the tribe. For him, things and the language of commerce do not allow themselves to be separated from the things and language of poetry. That is the lesson that he hurled steadily at [Théodore de] Banville with [the poem] "What is said to the poet concerning flowers." Rimbaud cannot consent to the elliptical syntax that, in advance, reduces the joy of the song. He also knows that a tribe evokes Israel, and that in the nineteenth century the tribe is called the people. He knows that "to incorporate" is properly "to incarnate" and that it is in the literature of the mystics that fires gleam on precious stones. He knows, in short, that there is no place of the poem that is separate from language in its entirety, from language and the utopias of language that charge it with promises of salvation.

That in fact is Rimbaud's great singularity. Before him poetics existed. Baudelaire still had at his disposal the great dictionary (of rhymes and fables) that made the very newness of "correspondences" possible. After him Mallarmé will invent the pure act of the poem. New poetry for Rimbaud must be identified with the whole of language. His fate is necessarily linked to the utopia of the new language and of reconciled bodies. Rimbaud travels through this utopia and undoes it by accompanying it with the other music: the speech of the uncounted, the idiot romance of obscure misfortune. In mourning for the new language of glorious bodies he shapes an idiom: not a dialect, but the opposite of a dialect. Rimbaud's idiom, identical to his poetry, is a paradoxical language, a "particular common" language, particularly common. Rimbaud makes its accents resound between the trumpet and drum of the popular song and the dialect of the idiot. He invents the poem without any place other than the totality of language, traveled by the idiom of the encounter always missed, the particular timbre of obscure misfortune.

## Logical Revolts

Rimbaud does not belong to the avant-garde. He does not take the plunge from old economies of salvation to new economies of production. He stays inside the gap between the old history—the song of the people and the salvation of bodies—and the new one, that of the poetical and political avant-gardes. He insists on singing of the unredeemable part of the economies of salvation whose music endlessly sells the dream of the glorified body.

A singular insurrection in language is born. We can name this insurrection (a few principles of which I have tried to isolate) with an expression drawn from *Illuminations*: logical revolt. As we know, the text says "We will massacre logical revolts." This "we" whose slang muffles the drum is that of the "soldiers of good will," the colonial armies of democracy that set off for disease-ridden swamplands. Of course, we also hear in the background the royal "we," by which the poet makes himself too a killer of logical revolts, and puts an end to the insurrection of his poem.

To give the poem its place and this massacre its intelligibility, it would be fitting to make it a panel in an altarpiece where it might join "Génie," the poem of the glorious poetic body, and "Solde," the poem of priceless bodies for sale. "Démocratie" is the poem of logical revolts massacred, of slang that stifles the drum; it is the poem in which the idiom of the poem is lost. If *Illuminations* needs an ending, it is not one poem alone that can form it, but only this triptych that redeploys the utopia of the poetic body and the counter-utopia of its completion. But to make this end intelligible, it must be framed between two declarations of principle, taken from two "poetic arts," one of which seemed pure amusement. The "serious" declaration is Mallarmé's: "Speaking has to do with the reality of things only commercially." The amusement is young Rimbaud's, advising Banville to become:

Shopkeeper! colonist! medium.

The trinity of the shopkeeper, the colonist, and the medium is precisely the one offered us by "Solde," "Démocratie," and "Génie." The seeming boyishness of the adolescent poet precisely fixes his poetic and personal destiny. Rimbaud has taken language seriously, he has taken the "reality of things" seriously. He has made himself shopkeeper and colonist, for lack of being a "medium" or a "génie," for lack of accepting a language of poetry that bids adieu to the ordinary reality of commerce, to the extraordinary reality of salvation, and to the singularity of mendicant childhood. He has made gold from colonial trafficking, for lack of cheating on the gold of language. He has in advance said goodbye to the avant-gardes, to the chisellers of poems and to the leaders of the parties of the glorious future, after having played his role, made the song of obscure misfortune resound in the logical revolt of his poems and his prose.

# PART II

*Theologies of the Novel*

# ONE

# The Body of the Letter: Bible, Epic, Novel

"The novel," it has been repeated since Hegel, "is the modern bourgeois epic." It is, Lukàcs notes, "the epic of a world without gods." How should we understand these phrases? Hegel's is already somewhat enigmatic. For he explained to us at length that the epic occurred only on the basis of a particular world, the "heroic" world whose characteristics are the exact opposite of the ones that define the modern bourgeois world. In the collective universe that Homer sings, the activities of men are not objectified outside them as laws of the State, as industrial methods of production or the workings of administration; they remain ways of being, and of individuation, character traits, feelings and beliefs. The epic poem reflects this "originally poetic milieu" where modes of activity are not separated from individuals, fragmented into forms of rationality separate from ethics and economics, from technology and administration. The novel, on the other hand, has as a presupposition, and as essential subject, the separation of characteristics, thoughts, and individual behavior from the objectified world where laws of family morality, economic profitability, or social order reign. In contrast to the epic, which was the poetry of an already poetic world—of a world unaware of the separation between the methods of *making*—the novel has the obligation of re-poeticizing a world that has lost its poetic character.

Isn't a bourgeois epic in fact a contradiction in terms? The individual's struggle against the bourgeois world can actually define only an anti-epic. No epic hero struggles against his world. And no poet would know how to re-poeticize a depoeticized world. To give consistency to the Hegelian formula, Lukàcs must apply to the novelistic genre—as a modern literary genre—the characteristics that Hegel gave to "Romantic" art, that is to say art founded on the Christian separation between individual subjectivity and an absolute that deserted the world with the body of the resurrected Christ. For Hegel, Romantic art is "Christian" art, an art in which no figure can adequately represent the divine since individuality cannot recognize in any object of the world the divinity that lives in its heart, because it is ceaselessly tossed back and forth between an essential interiority that does not find any reality fully adequate to it, and the multitude of adventures and encountered figures that mark the path of this impossible quest. The novel is then the modern "epic" because it is the epic of totality that is lost but still striven for. Novelistic "modernity" inherits as content the Christian distance between the individual and his god. "The novel is the epic of a time when the extensive totality of life is no longer given in an immediate way, of a time in which the immanence of meaning in life has become a problem but which nevertheless has not stopped striving for totality."

But this theology of the novel immediately reveals another paradox: the separation of individuality in the novel contrasts with this immanent relationship of individual action with the meaning embodied in a collective *ethos*. But from where precisely does this insistent idea of the epic as collective poem, poem of a meaning immanent to life itself, come? The epic, Hegel says again, is the Bible, the book of a people's life. But how is this Bible itself conceived if not in relation to the Christian philosophy of incarnation, to the idea of the Book that comes to life, of the letter that delivers its spirit by the action of a body? In short the "Christian" novel of the soul dissociated from the world is opposed to the living poem, in the incarnate sense of the epic. But this sense itself came to the epic only retrospectively, responding to the Christian opposition between the dead letter and the spirit that becomes flesh and blood. There are two "Christianities" then to be confronted in a paradoxical vein: a Christianity of incarnation that finds its realization in the pagan "Bible" of the epic poem, and a Christianity of absence that founds the "modern" epic of the novel.

So a strange theological-poetic circle comes to circumscribe the relationship of the novel with its ancient "model." The modern epic can be the replacement of the epic as well as the anti-epic. And the "Christianity" that animates this "modern epic" itself has two symbols: meaning incarnate in the body of Christ, or meaning withdrawn from the empty tomb. The ancient and the modern, Christian and pagan, the Old and New Testament dance around the novel to conceptualize a ballet in which terms keep changing place and signification.

It is within this complex pattern that Erich Auerbach's reasoning is inscribed, in *Mimesis*, in order to reflect on the genesis of realism in the novel, especially his recourse to the exemplary episode in the Gospel according to Saint Mark, the story of Peter's denial. Auerbach opts to read the Lukàcsian definition backwards: the novel, as modern—realist—genre of literature, is possible beginning at the moment when the "totality of life" is no longer given in merely the extensive dimension of actions situated on one single level, but in which the intelligibility of gestures, words, and events recounted passes by a vertical relation to a background that arranges them in dramatic perspective and as a destination of humanity. This vertical relation is peculiar to transcendental religions, and is exemplarily accomplished in Christianity, which is not the religion of the empty tomb, but of transcendence materialized in ordinary life, of the Word incarnate, giving the spirit its flesh and the body its truth. This point of view for Auerbach is what allows us to found the tradition of novelistic realism because it alone allows us to break the taboo that the Aristotelian division of poetic genres placed on such a representation. That tradition in effect classed genres according to the dignity of subjects represented. Elevated genres—tragedy or epic—suited only elevated characters, kings and heroes. The representation of lesser people was the job of low genres, comedy and satire. And Auerbach presents the story of Peter's denial as a counterpoint to two stories that mark the limits of the power of representation in ancient literary tradition. Caught in a division of genres that reserves noble genres for great characters and low genres for the representation of lesser people, it can describe the world of little people only as material for the picturesque. It can never read there the profound dimension of a common story. It is these limits that enclose Petronius describing the heterogeneous entourage of the freed Trimalchio, or Tacitus repeating as a rhetorical exercise the harangue of the rebel legionary Percennius to the troops in Pannonia. Neither of the two can see in the bearing of the little people he imitates the profundity of a story affecting all levels of a society. The tale of Peter's denial, however, introduces us to the familiar universe of little people: Peter who comes to warm himself at the fire, the soldiers, the maidservant who questions him and notices his Galilean accent. But this realistic representation is no longer for comical ends or rhetorical illustration. It is a dramatic representation of the life of a people taken with the extraordinary quality of the event. The realism of description is devoted to the event of the incarnation, to the presence and suffering of the Word, son of God, who fulfills the Scriptures. And it represents to us in the figure of Peter the man of the people divided between faith, disappointment, and fear, actor of a new spiritual movement who in his profundity grasps the world of little people. This adequation of an historical spiritual movement with the method of representation that shows it in its material density fractures the separation of subjects and genres. It makes possible the realism of the novel, whose principle is not so much the exact representation of "reality" as the dissociation of the grandeur unique to writing from the issue of the social dignity of the characters represented.

So Auerbach attacks tradition from the rear: the epic is not the chronicle of a people. Homer has no way to give a serious and tragic quality to the figure of Thersites. Nor can he give the representation of the life of Achilles or Agamemnon its human depth. With the story of Peter's denial, with the weight of perceptible signification unique to the Christian incarnation, the true "life story" that is the novel is founded.

Auerbach's analysis includes only one problematic presupposition. It postulates that the exemplary function of Christian narrative for literature comes from the fact that it itself is a factual account foreign to any literary intention: "The narrator's gaze does not skim over reality in order to arrange it rationally, nor does the account conform to an aesthetic intention. The visual and sensory element that appears here is not a conscious *imitatio* [ . . . ] this element manifests itself because it is inherent to the events recounted, because it is revealed in the attitude and words of beings who are profoundly touched, without the author making the least effort to objectify it" (1). Auerbach thus makes two "simplicities" agree with each other. The story of Peter's betrayal describes the heartbreak of a man of the people divided between two simple feelings before the great tragedy of the Passion: fidelity to the Messiah, and the disappointment of someone who expected of him an immediate earthly Advent. To this psychological realism of content corresponds a realism of form that is, in fact, the absence of form. But the writer is not a writer. The description he gives of Peter's deeds and words is a direct expression of the same spiritual and popular movement that provoked Peter's faith and denial. Mark can only be a witness who tells simply what was done and said in order to transmit it to the simple people at whom the message of the Christian spiritual revolution is aimed.

But to maintain this position Auerbach must forget what he nonetheless knows better than anyone: the "events" in question are not simply facts recorded by a witness; they are events that were announced in advance, events whose textual economy of Scripture already anticipated "concrete" reality. The scene of Peter's denial does obey an explicit intention: it shows that the Messiah's word that foretold his denial to Peter was indeed fulfilled. But the Messiah had made this anticipation of events to come itself the confirmation of a saying of the Old Testament. Peter had to deny Christ so that Ezekiel's prophecy could be fulfilled: "I will strike the shepherd and the sheep will be scattered." In short, the episode of Peter's denial enters this figural economy that perceives in the prophecies and stories of the Old Testament "figures" of the story of salvation, prefigurations or "shadows" of things to come, shadows become truths by the becoming-flesh of the divine Word. And the "realist" power of Christian narrative, this power it communicates to the novel narrative, is linked to this figural economy that inscribes the concrete event in an economy of the text, in a relationship of the text with itself. The heart of Christian/novel realism is this power of the figure, which is no longer the illustrative ornament of discourse or the allegory of a hidden truth, but a body announcing another body. The physical force of the scene of Peter's denial is due to this economy of the text that makes it an *a contrario* demonstration: the very denial of the Messiah because he announced it, because Ezekiel had already announced it, proves he is indeed the Messiah announced by the Scriptures. The Christian/novel realism of the scene comes from the overlapping of two things: the *poetic* figurative power, that of description that gives flesh by concrete notations of the universe of ordinary people, the fire where they come to warm themselves, the telltale accent of a voice, and the *theological* figural power that registers this little tale of simple things happening to the simple in the great economy of salvation where every little scene takes on the meaning of the truth that a "figure" has already announced and preceded.

But in order to assert the "non-literary" quality of Mark's narrative, Auerbach must separate these two powers. He splits the concept and use of the figure in two. He retains the benefit of the figural interpretation, that "spiritualization" of the popular body that makes it representable by breaking down all hierarchy of subjects and genres. But by retaining the benefit of the effect, he dismisses the cause: at the end of the same chapter, he contrasts the artifice of later figural exegesis, implemented by Church scholars to adapt the Christian message to the mental universe of the pagan world to be conquered, with the realism of the simple Evangelical narrative. In the Evangelical text he arbitrarily distinguishes a core of experience lived by the fishermen of Galilee and retransmitted by an artless narrative, from a figural interpretation added later on by the learned. Thus he goes back to the Feuerbachian tradition of reading the religious text, the one that grounds the mystery of speculative interpretation in its actual human content. The problem with this type of interpretation is, of course, that the "reality" that serves as standard is itself so only through the very speculation from which one claims to free it.

So we can imagine reversing the game. Auerbach bases a theory of realist novel on the becoming-flesh of Christian narrative. We can propose an opposite relationship. We can show that the event of flesh is first of all an event of writing, a production of writing by itself. And on that we can base a theory of the novel as game. That is what Frank Kermode does in *The Genesis of Secrecy*. Not that he is preoccupied with refuting Auerbach. But he finds in the same Gospel of Mark and in the same episodes of the Passion a model of novelistic practice that is the exact opposite of Auerbach's analysis: no longer on the side of the idea that becomes carnal presence but, conversely, on the side of the illusion by which the proposed carnal presence vanishes into the economy of the text. It makes this a simulacrum of a sacred text in which the novelist exercises his power to make the meaning it hides sparkle, a meaning that is finally nothing other than the pure relationship of writing to itself, the pure demonstration of the power of the writer.

Kermode's demonstration draws on another episode of the tale of the Passion. This tells us the story of the young man arrested at the same time as Jesus and who runs away naked, leaving his white linen tunic in the soldiers' hands. We find it hard to ascribe this isolated event concerning an unknown character to a simple eyewitness account. So we begin to think that its seeming insignificance relates to some other episode that gives it meaning. The most credible interpretation links the figure of this fugitive with that of the young man in a white robe whom the holy women find sitting next to Jesus' empty tomb. The abandoned clothing is then associated with the shroud in which Christ had been buried. And this interpretation is vouched for by the texts of the Old Testament, which give a prefiguration of it, beginning with the clothing abandoned by Joseph in the hands of Putiphar's wife. The episode of the young man in the linen tunic then enters a "hermeneutic in-

trigue." It is the sign indicating to the reader the necessity of a figural reading that looks beneath the story for the meaning that another story will reveal. This type of signs corresponds to those that the modern practice of the
novel uses. And the episode of the young man in the linen tunic finds its exact counterpart in Joyce's *Ulysses*, in the episode of the burial of Paddy Dig-
nam, where there appears an enigmatic man in a mackintosh who has no
function in the story, who is simply one of those innumerable enigmas that
Joyce says he composed "to keep professors occupied for hundreds of years."

The consequence of the figural narrative for the idea of literature then
takes on an entirely different significance. The Gospel of Mark is no longer
the account transmitted to the simple of what other simple people have
seen. It shows the fulfillment of the Scriptures. The story of Peter's denial
belongs to a hermeneutic intrigue that is supposed first of all to prove the
harmony of Scripture with itself. And this intrigue aims to separate those
who know how to unravel intrigues from those who do not know how. The
Gospel narrative, as literature and as a model for all literature, has the function of separating those for whom it is intended from those for whom it is
not intended. Kermode consults here the strange commentary that the
Gospels of Mark and Matthew give of the parable of the Sower. In this
parable, Christ in fact says to the apostles, taking up a passage from Ezekiel:
"To you has been given the secret of the kingdom of God. But for those on
the outside, everything is given in parables, so that they see and do not see,
so that they hear but do not understand." He sees in this "theological" program the model for a "poetic" program, the model for a literature in which
"stories are obscure" because the very skill of the writer is the *muthos*, the
plot of Aristotelian knowledge, but an intrigue of knowledge that the strategy of the sacred text has taught to become more complicated: it no longer
opens onto the fictional secret, the revelation of what the characters were
without knowing it. It ends—and hides—in the demonstration of the secret of fiction, of fiction as deployment of a secret that is nothing other
than itself.

Another theology of the literary body is thus asserted in which every story
of incarnation is the realization of a hermeneutic intrigue, in which every
display [*monstration*] is a way of hiding. A certain idea of literature is legit-
imized by it, one that Kermode illustrates by the Jamesian secret and the
Joycean enigma, one that could find its other paradigms in the genesis of the

poem in Poe or in the Borgesian labyrinth. The "infinite book" is here the image of the Scriptures: closed on the master's secret, hidden like the meaning of the parable and the pattern in the carpet, open to the infinity of interpretations and misinterpretations. The writer appears in it like a god, master of games and meanings, choosing those to whom he communicates the spirit of his book and those to whom he abandons its letter: literature as infinite autodemonstration of the powers of closure of the literary secret, which is also to say, the interminable elaboration of the image of the writer. Faced with the Auerbachian bias that naturalizes incarnation and paganizes the Christian relationship of the text to the body, this bias refers this very relationship back to the Talmudic midrash, the infinite relationship of Scripture to itself.

We can, then, construct two theologies of the novel, two conflicting interpretations of what the novel owes to the Christian equivalence of the incarnation of the word and the fulfillment of the Scriptures. One is based on incarnation and on the plenitude this confers on the representable body of literary narration; the other draws on this relationship of Scripture with itself that alone proves to be completely figuration. The mastery of the writer making every relationship of letter to letter into spirit and body is thus contrasted with the realist plenitude of the represented. But perhaps these two theologies of the novel are too easily freed from the knot of the problem: from the very precariousness of the coincidence between the truth of the book that is accomplished and the truth of the word that takes flesh. The model that the novel finds in the stories of the Passion could actually be neither the account of meaning embodied in the bodies of the humble, nor the sovereign word that creates a plot from the proffered/hidden secret of the Book. The connection of the novel to the chronicle is given to us neither in the bare representation of the heartbreak of the man of the people nor in the coded parable of the man in the white tunic. It is not in any fortunate relationship between the attestation of the text and the attestation of the body. For this fortunate relationship does not exist. The loop of textual proof and corporal demonstration is endless. There must always be a body to prove Scripture. There must always be Scripture to prove that the body in question is indeed that body. There must again be a body to prove that the body that disappeared was indeed the one that erased all distance of Scripture from itself. The certainties that are drawn from the little scene of Peter's denial or from the endless parable of the young man with the white tunic, contrast with the endless iteration that characterizes the "apocryphal" ending of the Gospel of John, the ending that, from addition to addition and from testamentary references to little picturesque scenes, ceaselessly proves that the one who writes the text is indeed the one that the Resurrected chose to bear witness to his Resurrection and to those thousands of other deeds of the incarnation whose written account the whole world would not be big enough to contain.

It is this very tension that for centuries will characterize two ways of thinking about the body that must give the story of the fulfillment of the Scriptures the supplement of truth that it needs. To bring out these two ways is to discern two relationships of the written to the body, two relationships of presence to absence, two theologies of the body of truth of Scripture. These two theologies carry the potential of two kinds of opposing poetics of the novel, two ideas of the relationship between the body of writing and the body of fiction.

## The Ark and the Desert

Let us try, then, to define these two ideas of the body of truth of Scripture to see how opposing poetics are deduced from it and how the interpretation of a novel's reality—and perhaps the reality of literature with it—has to do with the conflict of these two poetic theologies. The field of Christian interpretation of Scripture is defined by four notions, those of the spirit, the letter, the word, and the flesh, which are arranged in a proportion: the letter of Scripture is transformed into spirit in the same measure as the word takes flesh. It is in the interpretation of this proportion that I will isolate two interpretative methods that I can summarize, for convenience, in two sentences, one taken from Saint Augustine, the other from Tertullian. Saint Augustine's tells us this: "I could rightfully call Noah a prophet since the very ark he built and in which he and those belonging to him were saved was a prophecy of our time" (*The City of God*, XVIII, 68). Tertullian's says: "If flesh is fiction as well as its sufferings, the Spirit is falsity as well as its miracles" (*The Flesh of Christ*, V, 8). I would like to show how these two sentences present two interpretations of the body of writing that are prolonged into two theologies of the novelistic body. The first authorizes a coincidence between the theological body of the letter and the poetic body of fiction.

That is to say it makes a theory of truth incarnate coincide with a theory of creative imagination. The second separates these two bodies, isolating both the novelistic and literary singularity from any body of truth.

Let's start with Augustine's phrase. This can seem insignificant. But here it is a matter of one of the first episodes of a theoretical subject that will have numerous revivals: the dispute on the "wisdom of the ancient Egyptians" and its relationship with Jewish revelation. In fact this text is answering the pagan theory according to which Moses was Egyptian or, in any case, initiated into that famous Egyptian science, a sacred science hidden in the secret language of the hieroglyphs, but also an astronomical science a hundred thousand years old, much more ancient and venerable than the knowledge recorded in the sacred books of the Jews.

Saint Augustine opposes that view with a simple argument: an attested science exists only where a system of writing preserves its operations. But no book could have preserved those calculations made a hundred thousand years ago since the writing allegedly given to the Egyptians by Isis is no more than two thousand years old. Concerning the Hebrews, on the other hand, the anteriority of their science is attested by the anteriority of their writing. But how is this anteriority itself attested? Saint Augustine gives this question quite a remarkable answer: there has been writing as long as there has been prophecy. The inscription of a word summons a body to come from its truth or a figure proven by its later fulfillment, according to the interpretative procedure that Christian exegesis contrasts with ancient allegory: a figure is not an image to be converted into its meaning, but rather a body announcing another body that will complete it by making its truth corporeally present. Now the writing-prophecy of the Jews, according to Augustine, begins well before the prophets designated as such, well before even Moses and the exodus from Egypt. It is already at work in the acts of the patriarchs that Genesis tells us about. The materiality of these acts is already a writing since it prefigures the events of the Redemption to come. Noah was a prophet *because* the ark he built prefigures the story of salvation, accomplished by the coming, the death, and the resurrection of Christ. The thing can be put in the form of a syllogism:

> The ark is the work of Noah.
> But the ark is a prefiguration of salvation.
> So the work of Noah is the prefiguration of salvation, therefore it has the scriptural structure of a prophecy.

Obviously, the syllogism takes its force from something other than the linear sequence of its propositions—by joining three distinct acts into one single procedure of meaning: the discursive act of the holy writer telling the story of Noah; the technical act of Noah building the ark; the act of prefiguration that the story of Noah building his ark constitutes in the retrospective economy of sacred history. For Noah, to be a carpenter and a prophet is thus the same thing, as to be the object and subject of writing is also the same thing. To tell (the story of Noah), to make (the ark of Noah) and to prophesy (the salvation), all that makes only one single operation, precisely the operation of *representing*. Saint Augustine joins two effects of reality in this notion: the effect of materiality (the work of the ark) and the proof of the figure by its completion. The ark is not an inert construction of a craftsman. As prophecy, it is a word, animated with the life of the spirit. But conversely it is not a word that vanishes in the breath of language. It has the material solidity of things that art has produced. The fabricated object and the recounted narrative are, in their indissociability, prophetic writing, one single promise of meaning. The text is *already* of the body, the fabricated object is already of a language that bears meaning. The figure is the bearer of a double reality: the *figurative* reality of its material production and the *figural* reality of its relationship with the body-to-come of its truth. It is enough, then, to make one function slide under the other to transform the religious text into a poetic text or the coded narrative into the speech of life itself. That is what Auerbach achieves by annulling the distance of writing, by making the Evangelist's act of writing, and the emotion experienced by his character, two expressions of the same spiritual movement penetrating the depths of the people.

This operation is then inscribed in the long history of the theological-poetic transfer validated by the recovery of the figural and the figurative. The principle of this transfer is simple: make the figural function glide beneath the figurative function to transform, without blasphemy, the religious text into a poetic text. On one hand the figural vanishes beneath the figurative: the prophet is poet. The truth of his prophecies is the truth of the imagination, which speaks the figured language of images. But this disappearance of the figural beneath the figurative discreetly transmits its power to it, the power of attesting the truth of a body. The figural is "just" the figurative. But the figurative is still secretly part of the figural. It is under the sign of this double operation that the exegesis of the sacred text and the reading of the poetic text merge in the Classical age, in one single theory of the language of images and fables. The man who sums up this equivalence in the modern era is Vico. It is obviously not irrelevant that the motive of his research was the same as the one that guided Augustine: the polemic against the old philosophical and pagan illusion of the hidden secret of ancient fables. The theory of the "true Homer" refutes the notion of allegorical wisdom embedded in his poem. The fables and figures of the poet are only a language of childhood. But for that very reason, they are a true language: the language in which a youthful people expresses its awareness of itself and of the world, the language through which the long path of divine revelation enters the world. Homer is indissolubly theologian and poet. But his individual voice is also the voice of a people, gushing out from the very heart of its sensory experience. The Homer of the Christian Vico is then fully similar to the Jewish prophet of the atheist Spinoza. That is in fact what Spinoza means to show: Jeremiah's prophecy is empty speech if it is considered as a divine message and a promise of the future. But it is a full speech as the work of his poetic imagination and of his pedagogical eloquence, as a manifestation of the child spirit and of the child-people that expresses the divine through the veils of story. Jeremiah in sum is the Homer of the Jewish people, the editor of a life story that is no longer the story of the Word announcing its coming but of the people that learns to know and know itself in the colorful language of symbol. The "sacred poetry of the Hebrews" and the epic of archaic Greece fall under the same figure of the poem, indissolubly aesthetic and hermeneutic. Thence the epic Hegelian model is founded, that of the "life story of a people," the book shaped in the sensory cloth of the community that is a moment of its acting, a manifestation of its belief in which the Christian idea of the word incarnate and the Vican idea of poetry as the language of origins can be linked with the Romantic idea of the song in which the soul of a people is expressed. But here too is established a twofold way of looking at the novel: depending on whether one contrasts the abstraction of the novel's situation with the separation between an individual and his world, or whether, conversely, one subsumes the imagination of the novel under the idea of the ability to embody fabulation.

But even before Vico a man of letters and a future man of the cloth had posed the equivalence of the powers of the novel's fable and the powers of the sacred text. In 1670, Pierre-Daniel Huet, friend of Madame de Lafayette, in order to justify the author of *La Princesse de Clèves*, published his *Traité sur l'origine des romans* [Treatise on the origin of novels]. Where do these novels come from, he wondered. And he gave an answer transposed from Aristotle. The existence of the poem, for Aristotle, arose from the natural and universal pleasure of imitation. That of the novel, for Huet, comes from the natural pleasure that the human mind takes in the tale, a pleasure that takes its irresistible power from its double origin. Making up stories is the pleasure of the child, of the ignorant one who can express himself and understand only in the language of the image. But it is also the pleasure of the refined person who is expert at enriching discourse through all the play of figure. Thus the pleasure of the novel was shared as much by the barbarian peoples of the medieval West as by the refined courts of the East. But what especially deserves our attention is the extension Huet gives to the concept of the tale. In this single concept, he puts three things in effect: the invention of fables, the play of sonorous material of language (in short the domains of the *inventio*, the *dispositio* and the *elocutio* fixed by rhetorical tradition), but also the invention of procedures for the interpretation of fables. Thus the exegesis of stories belongs to the same activity as their invention, to the same activity too as the art that brings them to life. Just as Noah is a prophet in his capacity as carpenter and in his capacity as character of a tale, the same art of making fabricates fables, makes language function in them, and gives them meaning. In the Noah's ark of fable, one single, unique figurative activity is at work. This is expressed equally in the metaphors of the Koran, the parables of Jesus, or the myths of Plato; in the allegories of the Holy Scripture and the imagistic morality of Aesop; in Talmudic or figural interpretations, the "African" passion for rhymes, the play of parallels in the Psalms or in the prose of Augustine. Thus the Catholic bishop easily likens parable or Christian symbolism to the free play of "eastern" imagination, to Talmudic exegesis or to pagan philosophical myth. The sacred writer has turned into a poet, the symbol into a symbolic play of language. But this disappearance is itself possible only because the "promise of body" of the figure has been incorporated into the matter of imagination to identify it with a promise of meaning: a promise included in the natural and material language that announces in its imagistic profusion a language of the mind.

The genre without genre of the novel lends itself, then, to the exact recovery of figurality and figuration, of the body of the letter and the body of fiction. The figural, present/absent in the figurative, makes the figurative an infinite reserve, an infinite capacity of the mind to produce at the same time images, consonances, fables and exegeses, to produce meaning in images. In such a schema, the novel is nothing other than the manifestation of a general poeticity of the human spirit. It is nothing other than poetry: manifestation of the polymorphic activity of the mind that is at the same time fabrication, fiction, figuration, ornamentation, and interpretation.

### From the Folly of the Cross to the Madness of the Book

But this direct consequence of an interpretation of the body of Scripture as a fictional body will be upset by the other idea of the relationship of the body to the text that Tertullian's sentence embodies: "If the flesh is fiction as well as its sufferings, the Spirit is falsity as well as its miracles." Tertullian recalls the "fictionality" of meaning that forms the limit of every exegesis of the condition of the truth of the life story: not only the incarnation of the word but its incarnation in a suffering body. This alone attests to the truth of the "shadows" or figures of the Old Testament. But this truth of the suffering body of incarnation is, in its turn, only the announcement of things to come. It needs to be completed to deliver all its truth. But this completion can only be produced by the interpretation that confirms each Testament by the other. There must always be the sacrifice of a new body to make the truth of a body of writing come. That is precisely what Saint Paul says: "I complete in my flesh what the sufferings of Christ lack" (*Colossians*, I, 24). This is not a "figurative" way of speaking about his illness. It recalls the principle that submits every figure to the condition of a truth that is the truth of suffering flesh. The truth of the suffering body of incarnation requires that there must always be a new body to sacrifice itself in order to attest to it.

To give Scripture this new body, its commandment, the "Come, follow me" of the summons must be taken literally. It must be taken in its naked literalness, not guaranteed by any symbolic body, and can be true only through obedience "to the letter," through the renewed devotion of a body that proves its truth. That, faced with the ecclesial theology of the sacrament, is what establishes ascetic theology, which was lived in the deserts of Egypt before being codified in the great treatises, in particular Evagrius Ponticus's *Treatise on the Monk* and John Cassian's *Institutes of Monastic Life*. To verify Scripture from this perspective is to give it body again so that the letter can once again take form, to turn it over to that suffering in which incarnation fulfills its promise. The very idea of writing is then displaced from the shadow/truth relationship to the relationship of a text to its mark on the body. Suffering is what makes the body the presentation of the text, the surface of inscription of the divine message.

This procedure of meaning is a procedure of rarefaction. To the figural and sacramental procedure that keeps adding meaning and form around the letter and image, it counterposes a practice in which the manifestation of meaning in a body is accomplished not only through the extenuation of this body, but also through non-meaning (the "folly of the cross"), in the risk of non-meaning. The truth of meaning can come only through one who has devoted his body to those ascetic exercises that are not just exercises of suffering but exercises of the absurd. These exercises that the lives and words of the Desert Fathers describe to us find their culmination in that "mystical madness" that Michel de Certeau analyzes and that is symbolized for him by the "madwoman" of the convent of the Tabennesiotes, the woman who through her silence and obedience has been reduced to a wretched creature, has thus wholly removed herself from the circuit of meaning, from all symbolization, and disappears the day her holiness is recognized. The literature of the desert systematically takes these practices of the absurd, which makes of the exposed body a surface for inscribing the truth of Scripture, and contrasts them with the interpretative practice that "inquisitively scrutinizes the Scriptures." It is not a question of examining Scripture to read in it the relationship of figures to their fulfillment. One must annihilate oneself and also annihilate one's claim to be an interpreter of Scripture, to let its truth come in the form, even if absurd, of wounding one's body. Scripture is proven through the sacrifice of a body to the word of life. But this sacrifice of a body is also what reduces all writing to the pure insane materiality of the written mark. In fact it is within the framework of this theology that the practice of copying manuscripts was introduced into monastic life. Before it was an act of transmitting treasures of ancient culture, the work of copying was first a pure labor of mortification. It is recommended in the chapter on exercises of mortification in *Institutions of Monastic Life*. The labor of copying, like basket weaving, is supposed to occupy the monk, to take him away from the danger of *acedia*, from that vacant spirituality that falls back into bodily sloth. Originally the content of what was copied had no importance. The copy, even if it was of a testamentary text, enters the exercises of the absurd by which bodies are bent to obedience to the divine word. A good example of this is the little story of the monk of Latin origin, threatened by *acedia* on his arrival in the Egyptian desert, and whom a local ascetic saves by entrusting to him the task of copying a Latin text of Saint Paul, while carefully hiding from him the fact that no one in the desert of Egypt could read it.

What consequence that concerns the body of the novel can we draw from this folly of the body exposed to prove the truth of Scripture? It recalls the "Christian" novel that Lukàcs elicited from the Hegelian definition of Romantic art: the adventure of the soul looking vainly in the hazards of the world for a divinity that has deserted it. And that novel's protagonist par excellence, Don Quixote, presents his madness as equivalent to the madness of mystics, offering their bodies for the verification of the message all the way to the limit of non-meaning. But the core of the problem is not the analogy between the madmen of God and the madman of chivalric romances. It concerns the relationship between the body of writing and the body of fiction, and, with it, the "truth" of fiction. The unhappy verification of books to which Don Quixote sacrifices himself contravenes the smooth transfer of the virtues of incarnation to those of fabulation. In place of the relationship of correspondence between Noah as character, Noah as prophet, and Noah as "writer," in place of the equivalence between Homer's fiction and his characters' and people's modes of being, a dissociation is at work: the power of writing is divided between the knight's misfortunes and the mastery of his writer. The novel is not, then, the enchanted world of storytelling. It is the place where writing is exposed for what it is, stripped of body. And this impossible incarnation of writing brings back into question the principle of reality peculiar to fiction itself. And it is this rupture between the body of the letter and the body of representation that the epic of the bellicose Don Quixote fictionally carries out, to defend the unfortunate princess, victim of the Saracens, the puppets of Master Peter.

Since the time of the German Romantics, the character and text of Don Quixote have been enthroned as the foundation of the modern novel and literary modernity. Cervantes and his hero appear like Homer and Ulysses presiding over the rite of the novel as modern epic. But it remains to be seen what precisely the literary tradition invented by the Romantics established, by its fascination with the fable of the madman whose dream clashes every moment against reality, and with the writer's game, who amuses himself with a fiction of which he asserts that he is, and is not, the father. In one sense, the general question of the suspensive existence of literature can be led back to a specific question: what link is there between Don Quixote's madness and the power of the novel that portrays it? In short what does this "madness" consist of, if we are not content to divide it, in the Romantic manner, between the representation of the ideal confronting reality and the creative "fantasy" surmounting that opposition? In the interpretation of the relationship between the madness of the character and the "fantasy" of the author, the whole question of the "theological-poetical" nature of the novel is at stake.

The immediate answer says that madness consists in not knowing how to distinguish reality from fiction, in taking one for the other. It is the optical illusion of one who, having worn out his eyes and his brain in books, hallucinates reality in order to find there what he has already read. That is the explanation that Cervantes offers us in the first lines of the story, and that the Romantics revived as the conflict of the ideal with reality, won by the latter at the expense of the hero, won back by the former in the "transcendent fantasy" of the novel. But the same Cervantes offers us several episodes that do not fit this schema. The most significant is that of the false encounter with Dulcinea and her ladies-in-waiting. Sancho strives vainly to make them so beheld by Don Quixote, who instead sees only what reality presents to him: three fat ruddy-cheeked and ill-bred peasants. In desperation, Sancho kneels down in front of the false Dulcinea. And it is only then that Don Quixote enters into the game. His madness then does not consist in *mistaking* the green cheese of reality for the moon in a book, but in *imitating* the act that the book makes a duty: to devote himself materially, absurdly, like the ascetic, to the truth of the book. Don Quixote is mad out of duty. And he is quite particularly so when he has to imitate the madness of his role models, Amadis and Roland. When Don Quixote, who has withdrawn into the Sierra Morena, decides to act the madman like his model Roland, Sancho tries to oppose him with the objection of good sense: Roland, deceived by Angelica, had reasons for losing his head, whereas Don Quixote has none. But Don Quixote sweeps aside this prosaic good sense: big deal, being mad out of grief! What is truly praiseworthy is to be mad for no reason, or rather for the sole reason that one has to be mad, out of faithfulness to the letter of the book. Don Quixote's madness consists of being the person who imitates without reason what poets make their characters do because of some reason, obedient to a principle of reality of fiction that is, in Ariosto's *Orlando Furioso*, the well-encoded logic of passion that makes Roland mad, faced as he is with the evidence of betrayal transcribed on the trees and the rocks in the figurative language by which the interwoven initials of Angelica and Medoro imitate the intertwining of bodies making love.

The comparison of *Don Quixote* with *Orlando Furioso* will allow us to discern that principle of reality of fiction better. In fact it is present in Ariosto on three levels. First it is the body of the letter, which outlines what it signifies, the amorous encounter. Then it is the body of the verisimilitude of fiction, which fashions as a story a recognized rhetorical and poetic *topos*: passion drives one mad, and passion that discovers the deception of the other makes one superlatively mad. Finally it is the social body of the readership of the fiction, which validates the impossible nature of the madness as psychologically plausible, yet belonging to the category of what happens only in fiction. This social body is itself fictionalized as a condition of the poem. The poet represents himself as in the privileged position of a storyteller who is addressing a literate audience and in its honor unfolds an imaginary space-time of the poem in which each song is like a session, in which the poet plays with the attention of his audience and establishes in this very play the specific reality of fiction as a shared story. Between the materiality of the figurative writing that renders mad, and the materiality of the social body that institutionalizes the situation of fiction, Ariosto establishes the circularity of a reciprocal attestation. The poem is thus taken wholly in the logic of the overlap of the figural and the figurative. A passage from *Orlando Furioso* illustrates this slippage that makes the imagination of the profane poem overwhelm the reserve of the sacred narrative. When Astolpho, in imitation of Ulysses and Aeneas, descends into the underworld, the character who welcomes him there and sings to him of the glory of poets is none other than John the Evangelist. John begs him not to be surprised at his enthusiasm for poetry:

> I love writers and I share their lot
> For in your world I was a writer myself [ . . . ]
> And it is true that the Christ whom I praised
> Grants me reward for it.

This transformation of the evangelist into a court poet, expecting reward for his praises of his patron, might seem a singular blasphemy. But blasphemy, like madness, is included, defused, in the takeover of the figural by the figurative. And this takeover inscribes fiction in an assured principle of reality. Fiction forms part of reality as a particular space-time in which socially acceptable laws (passion drives one mad) produce fantastic consequences with which one can amuse oneself without trouble, since they do not go beyond the imaginary situation.

The madness unique to Don Quixote is to break this principle of reality of fiction that the people of good sense who surround him assert. They all recognize a space-time of fiction that has its well marked-out and delimited place in reality. Thus the innkeeper evokes the pleasure of those interludes, during harvests, when one enjoys oneself by reading those tales of chivalry about which one knows they are stories from another time. That is still, in our time, the position of a certain philosophical wisdom with regard to literature: the Searlian wisdom of the convention of suspension of conventions that forms the category of fiction as the emission and reception of "non-serious" statements. Don Quixote's madness interrupts this wisdom, it opposes the principle of reality that limits fiction to one single thing, the bare truth of the book. This madness hangs on a fundamental question: what permits us to say whether a book is true or false? To the canon that allows honest literary diversions while forbidding books made of imaginary stories, Don Quixote poses this crucial question: what allows one to declare the falsity of books of chivalry? If they are not true, what books are? There then follows a long series of books and a long series of attestations to their truth, a classic series of proofs by which stories—the lives of saints as well as novelistic accounts: ancient testimonies, recognition by competent authorities, traces and relics preserved, examined, commented upon—were traditionally authorized. Before this web of attestations, the conclusion seems to impose itself: "To try to make someone believe that Amadis was not of this world, any more than all the knights of adventures with which stories are packed, is to try to persuade us that the sun does not give light, that frost does not make cold, that the earth does not support us."

In its seeming absurdity, the sentence tells us this: the world is not just made of perceptible, experienced equalities; it is also made of books, not of a conventionally shared "imagination," but of a continuum of books and attestations to the existence of what they discuss. How can one slice into this continuum without drawing out the entire chain that also includes the *chansons de gestes*, the ancient epic, and—if we continue where Don Quixote leaves off—the holy books themselves whose truth is caught in this tight web of accounts, relics, and authorities. For Cervantes' time is one when the great proof of truth, incarnation, is in the process of vanishing into the system of traditional attestations. Don Quixote's madness, like the mystical madness analyzed by Michel de Certeau, is then to replay the decisive proof: the sacrifice of the body that exposes itself to attest to the truth of the book. Don Quixote gives his body in order to attest to the truth not of the Book but of books in general, all those books that run fatherless through the world. For the sake of all these orphan books he reenacts the "folly of the cross," the ascetic madness of bodies exposed not just to suffering but to the absurd in order to attest to the truth of Scripture. In prosaic terms, we will say that the quixotic fable is the specific fiction of a quasi-body that comes to experiment with the problematic of incarnation, and to measure the distance of every truth of the book from the truth of the Incarnate Word.

But the question, as we have seen, is not to show that the madman of novels acts like the madmen of God. It is to witness the specific relationship between writing and fiction that is there revealed. Don Quixote's madness consists in doing without reason what Ariosto's characters do with reason. It is to break the principle of reality of fiction; in short it is to exchange the position of the character for that of the author. Such is the peremptory reason with which Don Quixote retorts to Sancho's curt logic: isn't Sancho somewhat naïve to think one must be madly in love to imitate the madnesses of love? And does he imagine that poets take the sublime qualities with which they adorn the beloved seriously? In brief, Don Quixote knows as well as Cervantes that Dulcinea is only the peasant Aldonda Redonço. But the problem is precisely that Don Quixote is not the writer but the character, that the solitude of writing that gives every license to the fantasy of the one is what creates the madness of the other. This disjunction distances the novel from the easy relationship between Noah the character and Noah the prophet, Peter the simple man and Mark the simple witness, between the poetic individuality of Homer and the ethical individuality of Achilles or Ulysses. In its place is established the disjointed relationship between the mastery of the writer who can play with any illusion and the madness of the character who knocks against all reality, between the kingship of the novelist who writes the book and the perdition of his character, or of the one who reads novels.

It would be tempting, then, to suggest a simple contrast between two theologies of the novel, the same, in short, that contrasts the reader of the simple tales of Mark with the interpreter of his hermeneutic intrigues. With the everyday substantiality of the imaginary we would then contrast the om-nipotence of the writer, master of games and illusions. We know how the Romantic age played with such an opposition: as against the epic life story, the novel is autodemonstration of the omnipotence of the writer. And we see clearly how this figure is lent support by the exemplary relationship that links the writer's parade of mastery in *Don Quixote* with the madness of his character. Faced with the madness of one who believes in books, the writer presents himself as a conjurer who manipulates belief. Sometimes he disap-pears behind the objectivity of his story, sometimes he asserts his paternity over it, sometimes he portrays himself as its simple copyist. He takes pleas-ure in stopping the story whose copy he has lost, declares he has found it again thanks to an Arabic manuscript found by chance, makes his hero visit the printing house where his story is printed; in short he varies his status and his relationship to his hero ad infinitum. Thus the writer's power is dis-played in these games by which he makes fun of his characters and of his fic-tion by the intermediary of that mobile and eventually vanishing character that the modern age will call the Narrator. The eighteenth century in En-gland, with Sterne and Fielding, or German Romanticism, with Jean-Paul, will delight in this game, to the point of identifying it as the very power of literature. The relationship of the master writer to the madman of the book thus produces an easy theology of the literary: that of the circular book, re-ferring indefinitely to itself, playing for itself and for the greater glory of the writer the role of two testaments endlessly verifying their harmony. It is this theology that Borges's paradox in "Pierre Ménard, Author of the *Quixote*" symbolizes, the story of the new version of *Don Quixote*, word for word identical with the old one, yet entirely different, since the voice that utters it and the world of this voice change the meaning of all its utterances. There is a certain theology of literary divinity here that goes from the romantic con-cept of the all-powerful "fantasy" to end up at the Borgesian circularity in which every fictional body is plunged into the infinite ricorso of the book upon itself. We must, I think, pass through this illusion of the sovereign lit-erary game to reach an understanding of the literary semi-corporality, to think about what links a stance of utterance, that of the narrator going back and forth between the inside and the outside of the book, with a socio-theological fable, that of the madman of the letter. The quasi-existence of the narrator is not simply what assures the sovereignty of the writer over the experimental quasi-body of the character whom he makes his hostage. It is also what links this "sovereignty" to the position of his character or hostage: one whose madness is to read books. This sovereignty has as strict correlative the position of any human being seized by writing, that is to say seized by the defection of any incarnation of the *logos*. The genre without genre of the novel is the place of writing where the myth of the pregnant word, of the living *logos* presenting its body, encounters not so much the reality of the world as the reality of writing: that of a bodyless word that attests to it, the "silent painting" of which Plato speaks, and which will set off to travel the world without a father to guarantee the discourse, and will turn right and turn left without knowing to whom it should and should not speak.

Against any facile theory of a god as master of stories, playing with the madness of his characters and the belief of his readers, the modern novel manifests this solidarity of the power of writing with the dispersion of the letter that travels the world without a body of legitimacy. And its story is also that of the inversion of the initial relationship of mastery, which becomes the subjection of literary absoluteness to any character whatsoever, to any "madman," caught in the trajectory of the silent and loquacious letter. With Cervantes' happy fantasy one must contrast the modern and painful versions of the fable of any person seized by the book and impelled by the will to incarnate it. Don Quixote is then no longer named Pierre Ménard but Véronique Graslin (3), Madame Bovary, Jude the Obscure or Bouvard and Pécuchet—men and women of the people seized and condemned by passion for the book and the will to live this passion. But this transposition does not just give one painful version of the joyous fable of the madman of the book. Its narration effectuates the reversal of the power of the writer over his hostage. This inversion is seen for instance at work in the most exemplary way between the initial moment when Flaubert, in the first line of *Madame Bovary*—that modern, ordinary victim of a book—makes the first person narrative absent ("We were studying when the principal came in . . . ") and the moment we don't dare call final when Bouvard and Pécuchet, having returned to the desk they should never have left, expiate their sin: of wanting to enact the truth of books instead of being content to copy them out. The problem is that, as the price of their sin, Bouvard and Pécuchet, by copying out all the stupidity of the world, strictly undo the logic of the Flaubertian oeuvre, which had struggled to triumph, line by line, over "stupidity," that is to say over the insignificance of the world's prose, of those silent lives from which the experimental quasi-bodies of his novel with their entirely similar and absolutely different language had been taken. The happy theology of the novel turns round then. The turning of writing back onto itself is not the enchanted game of the writer as master of illusions; it is the stupidity of copying that transforms all writing into non-meaning, the absurd exercise of the monk's mortification, transforming the divine word into a book that no one will read. The Flaubertian absolutization of literature is not the sovereignty of writing that makes art out of all non-meaning. It is rather the inversion of this sovereignty, the revelation of its secret. And this secret is not the glorious "pattern in the carpet" which symbolizes the master of fictions playing with the reader's desire. It is the constitutive contradiction of literature. This is rendered absolute by asserting the equal worth of every subject, with regard to the "absolute way of seeing things" that is called style. But this very absolutization takes all proper language, all pregnant speech, away from literature. It is not just the character/hostage who pays the price of the withdrawal of all incarnation. It is this style itself that asserts its absolute difference only at the cost of making itself indiscernible from the great prose—from the great stupidity—of the world. Far from any fortunate incarnation of the word as arising from some mastery of the secrets of narrative, literature knows its power as that of writing alone. It knows at the same time that this solitude is the best thing in the world to share, that is to say the thing least shared.

# TWO

# Balzac and the Island of the Book

There are two simple types of narratives of space, in which space and narrative harmoniously agree, according to two opposing kinds of logic.

There is the story of the character who goes from place to place until he finds the place or object for which he had set out. He could be a king whom a god's anger endlessly diverts from a return to his kingdom, a lover in search of his noble betrothed, a young scatterbrain who runs after wealth from town to town, a young man who goes from village to castle, driven by theatrical fancies, and who discovers, at his final stopping place, the secret of his adventures. In this narrative, spaces are made to be traveled, from stage to stage. At each stage new scenes are set for the delight of the reader. But each stage also, of course, presents an ordeal, a temptation, an illusion, that hold the traveler back and make him wander still more from his path.

The story of Ulysses, or of Chereas, of Gil Blas, or of Wilhelm Meister. Narratives of spaces, narratives of initiatory journeys, guided by their goal: the place where one arrives, not always wealthier, but in any case rich in wisdom.

Then there is the opposite figure, where space is the framework that surrounds the narrative, the environment that engenders the characters and their relationships. The scene is set first in an overall view. The lens then draws closer, discovers the characters and their story summoned by the setting; they reflect and put into action the properties that the place, as environment, determines. This could be Madame de Mortsauf, appearing like the lily of the valley first embraced by the gaze of the beholder. This could be, in [Hugo's] *Quatre-vingt-treize* [Ninety-three], the Chouans, children of the hedged farmland, who rise up from it, formed by it, similar to it. Or it could be the workroom in [Zola's] *Docteur Pascal,* illusory haven of scientific peace that its well-closed shutters try in vain to protect from the burning sun that surrounds it, from the law of heat and blood that will end up carrying him away and making the old scholar its prey.

We have two simple figures, then: the narrative that travels through its space, and space that engenders its narrative. Two fictional narratives, each differently suited to shape the framework of a scientific discourse, on sociology or history, for instance.

But I am interested here in a third type. In this narrative, the two elements are there, but they remain foreign, confronting one another, looking daggers at each other. There is a story of quest, of wandering and salvation, with the elements, then, of a narrative of the first kind. There is a framework of narrative, an environment that projects onto its characters its qualities of urban grayness or rustic coarseness. Only, the two terms do not meet up with each other. Instead of lending itself to the characters' journey or conferring its properties on them, space becomes frozen, fixed in one of its points, and it places there, as if across the narrative, a truth of the story which the narrative will henceforth chase in vain. There is, then, a middle of the milieu that undoes its properties. The truth of the place and the knowledge of the narrative can no longer coincide, or else can do so only by a show of violence, through which the author has to reveal himself openly, and which for Aristotle characterize bad plot, if not bad authors.

An example of this narrative of space is one whose first episode the journal *La Presse* offers its readers in the issue dated January 1, 1839. Its author is Honoré de Balzac, its title, *Le Curé de village* [The village priest], and the first episode is entitled "Christian Solicitudes." Now the story seems to begin well, narratively speaking. The first sentence places us on a hill that dominates the theater of the action to come: the terraced gardens of the episcopal palace of Limoges, overlooking Vienne. From there we contemplate, with panoramic gaze, the locale that encloses a story and must give the characters their characteristics. It is, then, apparently, a narrative of the second kind, introduced according to the rules of the art. But our panoramic gaze will suddenly find it is locked on a privileged perspective. Toward the west, beyond the outskirts, the description points out to us an island covered with poplars, whose shadows, at sunset, come to divide the river's waters and to reach an isolated house on the shore. On the last terrace where we go down with the two vicars looking for him, the master of the place is sitting, the bishop, whose eyes are fixedly staring at that line of shadow the poplars cast, which links the island to the shore.

The curates think the prelate is distracted. Not at all, the narrator tells us. "The prelate thought he saw in the sands of Vienne the word of an enigma that was being sought for by the whole town." Three times, then, this island has been placed under our gaze. And already we are told that a privileged gaze can foretell in it the word of the enigma, hidden in the island's sand. What enigma, exactly? The curates outline for us the business it concerns. A man condemned to death refuses to make a Christian repentance before the execution. On the contrary he bombards his confessor with shouts and obscene songs. It is a matter, then, of avoiding scandal for the Church. And the solution suggested is to go and look for the priest of the condemned man's village, an obscure holy man, Father Bonnet. Having made his decision, the bishop resumes his viewing angle, next to his young secretary, the Abbé de Rastignac, to whom he says these strange words: "The secrets of the confession that we seek are no doubt buried there." To which, no less strangely, the young priest responds: "I always thought so," reminding us in passing of a female accomplice who must now be trembling in some beautiful house in the town. We do not know what the secret in question is, nor why the young priest and his master have always thought it was hidden there. Thus the island, right away, focuses the narrative on its secret, this secret that the ecclesiastic gaze has already pierced, even before we know what is at stake and what the crime that has been mentioned is.

The rest of the story, of course, will little by little reveal the business to us. An old miser who lived in the isolated house beyond the outskirts of the town was robbed and killed, along with his female servant. The guilty man is soon found with the help of various signs: footprints on the scene, a buried key to the garden, a piece of his shirt in the trees. It is a young porcelain worker, Jean-François Tascheron, till then known for his irreproachable habits and conduct, fruits of his education by the priest Bonnet. But Tascheron retreats into a system of silence and refuses to say, not just the motive for his crime, but also the place where he has hidden the old man's gold. This strange behavior leads us to think that the motive is love and, probably, love for a person above his condition, whom the young man does not want to compromise. This silence, after his condemnation, is transformed into those shouts and obscenities that are the object of the "Christian solicitudes" and the reason for Father Bonnet's mission. The holy priest succeeds in his undertaking: Jean-François Tascheron dies as a Christian, which is good, and promises that the money will be restored, which is even better. The first part of the story can then conclude in the setting where it began. On the bishop's terraces, one fine autumn evening, another character is seated on the last terrace, looking in the same direction. Not the representative of divine grace, but one of human justice, the prosecutor from Limoges. It is then that, both literally and figuratively, an illumination occurs. The prosecutor's gaze is surprised by a fire on the island, and the light goes on in his brain. We have been imbeciles, he exclaims. The secret was there. And, in fact, it is indeed there, except that, when the envoys of justice arrive on the scene, they find the brother and sister of the condemned man, who have just unearthed the money hidden there in the sand, but also burned those pieces of cloth in which it had been hidden that might perhaps have led to an identification of the "female" accomplice.

In one sense, we know the secret evoked by the initial scene. But it is only the most immediate sense: the pile of money was indeed there. We still do not know the accomplice who could identify the motive for the crime. But above all, we still do not know the reason through which, by their gaze alone, the bishop and his secretary always knew that the secret was there. We do not know the reason for which, imperiously, the narrator positioned us across from this place of the secret and identified his gaze, guiding our own, with that of the priest, piercing the appearances of the flesh. What affair of the soul is there under these pierced appearances? In what way, and of what exactly, is the island the secret? Not just the hiding-place, but the secret of the story and the "soul" of the crime?

Then comes the second part of the novel, entitled "Véronique." After a somewhat laborious connecting piece, it begins as a narrative of space of the second kind in the great Balzacian tradition. The description of the sordid lower quarter of Limoges comes to focus on a particularly ramshackle hovel and describes the master of the house, who resembles it. Sauviat is a dealer in scrap metal from Auvergne who has, thanks to the sale of government property, made a carefully hidden fortune. Without changing anything in his lifestyle, for reasons of domestic convenience he married, late in life, a robust peasant who has given him a daughter, the girl on whom the tale will concentrate: Véronique, the soul and genie of the place, the "little virgin of the slums," a child remarkable for her beauty and her docility. Only two events will mark her youth. Smallpox will first of all ravage her beauty, without however destroying it completely. Sometimes, this beauty, withdrawn into her soul, comes to pierce the envelope of the flesh and illuminate her face. The second event is the purchase of a book, during a Sunday walk, at an open-air stall: *Paul et Virginie*, the epitome of all edifying books, whose acquisition the priest consulted can only highly praise. And yet, the narrator tells us, this extremely chaste book will, more surely than an obscene one, devastate Véronique's existence. By it "the veil that covered nature" will be brutally torn from her eyes. Véronique dreams of the tropics and of chaste loves. She takes pleasure in contemplating the island opposite her window. She rebaptizes it with the name of Paul and Virginie's island, the Ile de France. She fabricates a novel and imagines herself raising to the height of her ideal world one of the young workmen who pass beneath the windows of the Sauviat house.

These dreams, though, seem to return to order. On the priest's advice, the Sauviat couple set about getting Virginie married. And the scrap worker's secret fortune allows him to arrange the marriage with the banker Graslin, who is having financial difficulties. It is an unhappy marriage with an ugly, greedy husband, indifferent to his wife's aspirations. She consoles herself with reading the spiritual masters, with her salon, where she gathers together the most interesting people in the town, and with all kinds of pious works, aimed especially at the moral education of the factory workers. She seems to be satisfied with her fate, and to be drawing closer to her husband, by whom she is expecting a child soon. Here the story of Véronique comes to link with that of the crime. She is pregnant at the time of the trial, and Véronique takes up the cause of the young man, trying vainly to convince the public prosecutor, who frequents her salon and who, without listening to her, will request, and obtain, the death penalty. After the verdict Véronique is stricken with a grave illness which she barely survives.

The reader, of course, long ago stopped having any doubt about the identity of "the woman." He will see without surprise the recovered Véronique, a mother, but soon a widow, leave Limoges and settle on an estate that her husband had bought in the village where the priest and the murderer live. The novel's final part, entitled "Véronique in the tomb," places us, eleven years later, on another terrace, belonging to the chateau in this village of Montegnac. After a glance at an idyllic nature of green pastures and fat herds, fruits of the activity of the lady of the manor, the tale brings us into the interior of the house where Véronique is dying. Before dying, she makes a public confession in which she tells everyone this secret that is no longer so for the reader: it was to flee with her that the unfortunate Tascheron had committed this robbery that circumstances had transformed into a crime. Since the beginning of the second part we had "understood." But understood what, exactly? Not just the identity of the accomplice but also why the island had been the place of the secret. It is so because it is Véronique's island, the one she identified with the island in *Paul et Virginie*. If the treasure is found there—the fruit of the crime—it is because Véronique had placed her treasure and her heart there first, because she had localized her romance there, the romance into which she had led the young worker of her dreams, the unfortunate Tascheron. The island is the "scene of the crime" because it projects into the space of the action, it makes literal another island: the insularity of an island dream that is a sickness of the ideal, a withdrawal of a young woman from her condition. This withdrawal is the effect of an island story, a story fatal to young women of the people, not because of its coarseness, but, on the contrary, because of its ideal purity.

Such a moral to the story does seem somewhat limited. And it does not justify the singular structure of this narrative of the third kind, the focus on this island that suspends the narration, by identifying itself with a priest's gaze. One cannot stop there, and Balzac himself does not stop there. Once the serial publication was completed, the novel was supposed to come out in one volume. But the publisher had to wait more than two years for copy. And he will get it only by dint of a bailiff's summons. What was happening during those two years? Balzac made two important changes to the story. First he simply reversed the order of the first two episodes, now beginning with the story of Véronique's childhood and marriage, to lead to a parallel second part of the story about the crime and Madame Graslin. In fact, the novelist found himself facing a dilemma: the reader of the initial "Christian Solicitudes" had difficulty in seeing why he should come back from this obscure effect to the search for such an oblique cause. The reader of "Véronique," on the other hand, is informed so soon of the cause that he scarcely has any reason, once the effect has occurred, to wait for its revelation. By starting with the cause, rather than the prelate's gaze, Balzac chose the least illogical solution. But obviously he then makes the third part of the book even more superfluous.

That is when the second transformation occurs: now that this part has become even more superfluous, Balzac will stretch it out excessively. He of course has a good reason for that. The book is called *The Village Priest.* It is made to show the remedy for the sad transgressions it describes: Christianity practiced in all its purity, like a system that is not just spiritual but social, in opposition to the fatal social ideologies and transformations of the post-revolutionary century. The book must edify, then, showing the priest in his task of evangelization, and accompanying Véronique in her long expiation.

Only that is not what this interminable section actually does. If we put aside all sorts of secondary episodes, uplifting conversations or stories of penitent convicts, it is mainly filled with the story of the great works Véronique undertakes to fertilize Montegnac's dry lands. The priest's observations of the loss of water from the forested mountain have convinced him that it is possible to capture the water with a dam and to redirect it to irrigate the plain. And it is to these great works that Véronique devotes her capital, under the supervision of a young engineer who is disgusted with the State schools and influenced by the notions of Saint-Simon. The arid fallow lands thus become great pastures and ensure general prosperity.

Obviously the expected story, that of the priest's pastoral work edifying the village by the word of God, has been consumed by another, another story of space, once more defined by the perspective of a man of God, a man who proves to be so less through his word than through his gaze that pierces appearances, connects spaces, and sees, too, a hidden treasure where no one looks for it. The third part of the novel brings the remedy for the wrong done, not by teaching a doctrine but by constructing an alternative topography or geography, another relationship between land and water. To the island of dream and crime that lazily occupies the middle of the river is contrasted the great irrigation network that fertilizes the land. To a relationship of land and water in which two children of the people—a worker and a scrap metal worker's daughter—are lost is contrasted another relationship from which arises prosperity for the people of the countryside. Thus the third part does not contrast morality with vice or reality with the imaginary. It contrasts two geographies, in the strict sense of the word: two ways by which writing is inscribed in a space.

We can understand better, then, this island story. The island is not just the fiction within a book. It is the metaphor for the book in general, for the book as a type of being. The space of the island and the volume of the book express each other and thus define a certain world, a certain way in which writing makes a world by unmaking another one. To understand this, I will suggest a detour through another island story, belonging to another kind of literature, which we call "worker's literature." In 1844 the *Mémoires d'un enfant de la Savoie* [Memoirs of a child of the Savoy] appears, told by Claude Genoux, formerly a chimney sweep, who tried his hand at everything and traveled the world, before becoming a machine feeder at a printing press. In his preface, Genoux tells us how, at the age of sixteen, traveling by boat between Lyon and Marseille, he was forced by circumstance to spend the night on an island in the Rhône. "There," he tells us, "in a poor cottage where some bargemen gave me shelter, I found on a shelf a book half devoured by worms. This work, which had lost its title page, seemed to me to present the adventures and first poetic inspirations of a young man from Avignon named Léonard. Reading this book, full of action and emotion, brought me a most pleasant night. In the morning, when I had to leave and abandon this book that did not belong to me, and that they were not willing to give me, for it comprised, by itself, the entire library of these fine people, it seemed to me that I was leaving a friend for the last time."

Since then, he tells us, he has vainly sought to find this nameless book, forgotten by all except him. "Well," he adds, "instead of the oblivion into which this book has fallen acting to discourage me, it gave me on the contrary all the strength and will to write this book in the same genre. Perhaps, after my death, I told myself, some studious young man will also find my work on the shelf of a smoke-filled shack; perhaps he will keep its memory as I have kept the memory of Léonard." After which Genoux tells us about his travels and the more or less credible adventures that led him, along with a few others, to that most famous island of writing, Robinson Crusoe's.

It is clear that this tale is first of all an exemplary fable, the story of the encounter of a child of the people with the book. And the encounter is all the more exemplary since the book is unique, separated from all others, enclosed on an island. The island as a separate place and the book as a continent of insular words signify each other. This fable is the source of meaning in those inevitable scenes in autodidacts' tales, where the simple child of the people tells us the story, always the same, of his first encounter with the book, on an open-air stall, on a holiday, and on a harbor, preferably. All these island stories of the book and the book-island are too similar to each other for one not to recognize *muthoi* in them, in the Platonic sense of the word, tales of destiny.

The fable Balzac tells us belongs to those narratives of fate, where the island of the book gets in the way of the course of a life normally devoted to the work of manual labor or housekeeping. The "crime" comes not just from that story of a happy island Bernardin de Saint Pierre's book [*Paul et Virginie*] describes. It does not come from utopia as we ordinarily think of it, as a dream of distant islands where all relationships would be pure and transparent. The evil comes from the book in general, from this parallelepiped enclosing pages of writing that gets in the way of a life that asked only to continue on its straight course. It comes from this island of words that is the book, made of words that have been diverted from the usage of language suitable for those men and women whom a life of labor awaits. According to this usage, the word is borne by a body, addressed by one body to another, and designates states that have been experienced, or actions to be carried out. Every word has a well-determined point of origin and point of destination, and is thus inscribed in an ordered arrangement of bodies in their place and in their function. The trouble comes, then, when this space is riddled, pierced, by spaces with indeterminate destination: places for walking that are also marketplaces and where merchandise of a specific kind is available, words separated from their normal ambit, folded back into this volume of the book that is also, according to Mallarmé, transformed into a "spiritual instrument" or a "minuscule tomb of the soul." These words are taken from the normal play of speech that designates, orders, and designs. Hereafter, they are spoken by someone we no longer know to anyone at all. They outline a unique space that superimposes itself on the normal arrangement of bodies in a community and reorganizes the entire relationship between words and things, between the order of discourse and the order of conditions.

These tales of books found on islands or of islands where the evil spell of the book takes hold look like so many answers to a great fable, an originating tale, whose elements they redistribute and whose meaning they invert. I'm speaking of this originating tale that for more than two millennia has regulated thought about writing in the West, namely, the Platonic narrative at the end of *Phaedrus* that presents the inventor Thoth showing off his invention, writing, to King Thamos. You have found, the king responds, the means not to make people learned, but to make them into semblances of learned men, and wearisome people. In fact writing possesses a double fault. First, it is silent, like a painting that stupidly keep signifying always the same thing. It is incapable of traveling with the *logos* it outlines, to answer those who question it, so it is incapable of making this *logos* a principle of life, a power that can grow in the soul. Secondly, it is, on the contrary, too talkative. Not being a *logos* guided, accompanied by its father, it sets off anywhere at all, without knowing to whom it should and should not speak. Writing is thus silent/talkative painting, the orphan utterance, deprived of the voice that gives it meaning and legitimacy, diverted from the trajectory by which the *logos* is a principle of life.

Thought of this way, writing is not just an inferior mode of speech. It is an imbalance of the legitimate order of discourse, of the way in which it is distributed and at the same time distributes bodies in an ordered community. To understand the principle of this disorder, we have to go back in the *Phaedrus* to a previous myth, that of the cicadas, used to contrast two categories of beings: the workers who come, at that hot hour when the cicadas sing, to take their nap in the shade; and the dialecticians, separated from the former by the leisure of speech, of the living and limitless exchange of words. Even before that another myth, that of the winged chariot and the fall, had based on truth the distribution of souls in various conditions of life. It had in effect linked the inequality of incarnations of souls born in such or such condition to the capacity or incapacity manifested by these souls to bear the view of heavenly truths. The inferiority of a given condition thus revealed the indignity of a mode of life separated from true modes of *seeing* and *speaking*.

The disordering [*dérèglement*] peculiar to writing confuses this hierarchy, introduces dissonance into the communal symphony, which Plato thinks of as the harmony of three things: the occupations of the citizens, their ways of doing; their mode of being or *ethos*; and finally the communal *nomos* that is not just the "law" of the community, but also its "melody" or tone. By confusing the destination of living speech, writing confuses this relationship between ways of doing, ways of being, and ways of speaking whose harmony constitutes, according to Plato, the community animated by its living soul.

I suggest we give this disorder the generic name of literarity [*littérarité*]. It constitutes a graver challenge for thought, perhaps, than the disorders of poetic fiction and the unhealthy simulacra it places, according to Plato, in the citizens' soul. In fact, these word-islands that silt across the channeled river of *logos* are not content with troubling fragile souls. They re-carve [*redécoupent*] the space that is between bodies and that regulates their community. They outline, on the topography of the community, another topography. And this topography divides up the insular spaces of another community: the community governed by the letter and by its islands, that is to say democracy.

Democracy, in fact, cannot be merely defined as a political system, one among many, characterized simply by another division of power. It is more profoundly defined as a certain sharing of the perceptible, a certain redistribution of its sites. And what orders this redistribution is the very fact of literarity: the "orphan" system of writing, on reserve, the system of those spaces of writing that, with their overpopulated void and their overtalkative silence, riddle the living cloth of the communal *ethos*: the royal portico of Athens where the laws are written on movable tablets, placed there like stupid paintings, the *Politics* tells us, like prescriptions left by a doctor who has gone away for any illness that might come; the theater's *orchestra* where, Socrates tells us, anyone can buy, for a drachma, the books of Anaxogoras, Pericles' master, the physician who was the first to raise "the veil covering nature"; the Athens assembly hall where the power of one silent and talkative word is exercised, more suitable than any other to engender chatter, the word *demos*. We know that this word first meant only a territorial division: the area or corner of earth where one had one's roots. It changed its meaning after the reform of Cleisthenes, who, in order to break the power of the nobles, restructured the Athenian tribes by forming them into geographically separate *demes*, one from the city, one from the coast, one from the mountain. This reform didn't only change the representation of the city's territory by making it consist of separate islets. It also made the political figure of the *demos* emerge: the people, that is to say the collection of "people of no means," the void born from the inclusion of people of no means and from its identification with the totality of the community.

Democracy is first of all this topography of the "insular" community of writing. A topography that can be imagined as a shady marriage of earth and water. Democracy is the system of oarsmen for Plato, who dreams of establishing his city as far away as possible from any maritime influence. The system of the people is the system of writing, and it is also the system of the island. We ordinarily associate the image of the island with utopia, with the distant imaginary place. But it is first of all democracy whose representation the island symbolizes. Democracy is this "empty," "abstract" space that divides up the power of the few words available: people, equality, liberty, etc. It is also the movement by which these available words take hold of and divert from their intended path people who had not been concerned with dealing with *logos* or the community.

This confusion of lives diverted by the insular power of available words is, we know, an the obsession of Balzac's time. That is what was called in his time *déclassement*: the misfortune of working-class bodies torn from their natural goals by the course of the letter and thrown by it into ways of wandering and misery, suicide and crime. *The Village Priest* is an exemplary fable of democracy, that is to say of *déclassement* thus understood. In fact those are the givens of the fable. The Revolution overturned social conditions. It made Sauviat, the iron worker, a hidden millionaire. In Plato, the oligarch miser had prodigal democracy for a son, greedy to enjoy and vary its pleasures without hindrances. The metalworker's daughter is stricken with a subtler and more dangerous form of the democratic malady, the same one from which those "distinguished young workers" suffer, of whom the unfortunate Tascheron is the prototype. It is not money that interests them, but the gold of language and thought.

That is the crime of democracy and of the book, their symbolic crime, the denaturation of the working-class. The fable of the murder and the island transforms this symbolic crime into an actual crime. It is this literalization of the idea of the book that explains the bizarre qualities of the story. It explains the fixation of the gaze that crosses diegetic space and rests in a hallucinatory manner on the "cause" of the crime. It explains the novelist's difficulty in linking together space and the narrative, the fixed gaze that aims at the geometric scene of the crime and the logic of the judicial investigation. Here we can think of the strange quality of the logic of clues that allow them to arrest Tascheron: essentially traces of men's dress shoes and a key buried at the scene of the crime. Finding the key lets them find the one who provided the iron, the one who provided the file, and thus work back to the murderer whose shoes correspond to the footprints. It is a strange method of identifying a murderer. And it was, for the murderer, a strange notion, to bury the key instead of throwing it in the water. But it is a question of identifying not the person of the murderer but the race to which he belongs, that of metalworkers, and to reconstitute not so much the preparations for the crime as the other crime, the symbolic crime that preceded it, the one that made an ironworker take a walk in dress shoes at an hour when his co-workers devote themselves to a refreshing nap. In short, the sign also crosses the plane of diegesis to point directly, through the narrative, at the cause of the murder, the crime of democracy, the crime of the book that separated the scrap metal worker's daughter and the porcelain worker from their destination. The logic of place devours the logic of narrative. The logic of the fable and of its morality devours that of the fiction. It fixes the novelist on his terrace, in place of the one who sees and travels through the story toward its cause. This place is that of the priest, the seer. But the priest, the one who sees, is also the one who does not write. The novelist must write. He must lead his fable to the end of its logic.

But what exactly is the end of this logic? Or, which amounts to the same thing, what makes the third part interminable? It is not enough for the heroine to atone, put right and confess. The wanderings of exalted imaginations can no doubt also atone for themselves. But it is not a question of these wanderings. It is a question of the crime of the book, of the misfortune of writing. Good works will never be enough to expiate this misfortune. And no word, not even the priest's, can find a cure for it. No living word is enough to remedy the disorder of writing. The remedy for the misfortune of writing is another writing, a writing below or beyond words, that opposes their talk as well as their silence with another mode of inscription or circulation.

That is what the strange episode said long ago, which follows, in the *Phaedrus*, the story of the inventor Thoth and King Thamos. Phaedrus was being ironic about Socrates' unverifiable Egyptian stories. Socrates answered him with a curious argument: You young people, you're always showing off with your requests for verification of sources. Our ancestors, though, listened to the oracles of the god who expressed himself by the sound of the wind in the oaks at Dodona. And they didn't worry about the origin of the message, as long as it was true. Phaedrus didn't think it wise to add to his impertinence by asking Socrates how one goes about recognizing the truth of messages in the sound of the wind in the oaks. And, in fact, it is another idea of truth and of writing that is contrasted here with the restless wandering of silent-talkative words: a writing that is less than the written, a pure trajectory of breath—of spirit—communicated as the immediate respiration of truth.

But "good" writing can also be writing that is more than what is written, writing that is not written on papyrus, parchment, or paper, but is inscribed in the very texture of things, as an actual modification of the perceptible world. In Balzac's time, this utopia of a writing that is more than written is embodied in the ideas of Saint-Simon. To the "Protestant" system of writing, the Saint-Simonians contrast the new Book, the Book of Life of the new community. This book is no longer traced with signs on paper, signs that isolate men and build up phantoms of democratic politics. This new book is traced with the ways of a true communication, the ways of iron and water that actually link together men, their actions and their thoughts. When the Saint-Simonians go to Egypt, attracted by the dream of the canal connecting the two seas, Michel Chevalier contrasts this actual writing with the mystical and diaphanous ideology of political parties: "We trace our arguments," he said, "on a geographical map." And the "Book of Deeds" that relates the journey of the apostles of the industrial religion to Egypt exemplarily contrasts two writings, that of the old Egyptian priests who hid their thinking in their signs and that of the new engineer-priests. "In Egypt," the text says, "we will not decipher the old hieroglyphs of its past greatness. But we will carve into the earth the signs of its future prosperity."

That is the same writing that Father Bonnet, the engineer-priest, practices in Montegnac with his assistant, the science student Gérard. Balzac complains about his publisher who did not leave him time to show us Father Bonnet teaching the catechism. But Father Bonnet has better things to do. He has another script to put to use on his parish's land: those lines of water that inscribe on the soil of Montegnac "the signs of its future prosperity." The Catholic priest is first of all an engineer of souls in the Saint-Simonian manner, someone who changes souls by changing the mode of community between bodies by lines of industry traced on a territory. Similarly, the important thing is not that Véronique perform some work of charity or contrition, but that she renounce one writing for another, one course of water for another. "I have marked," she says, "my repentance in indelible lines on this earth. It is written in the fertilized fields, in the enlarged market town, in the streams directed from the mountain to this plain, which had previously been uncultivated and wild, but is now green and productive." The indelible lines, of course, are the opposite of the erasable letters of book-islands. The true work of expiation that atones for the crime of the book is the dam and sluices that distribute to the children of the people what they need. Not words, tenderness and dreams. Not even those words of Holy Scripture that an old nun had taught to Véronique and that were *already too much*. Not words, then, but water to fertilize their labor and their fields.

Putting such a demonstration into a book, and a novel, is obviously something of a paradox. And we can understand Balzac's difficulty in finishing his book and his dissatisfaction with the completed work. This book, he tells us, is "complete with regard to drama" but mutilated with regard to the moral. The modern reader might rather tend to think the contrary—that, as to the moral, there is more than enough, but that the drama, with its themes that contradict each other and its backwards order, seems defective. But both judgments can be in agreement. For how could the moral be perfect and the book completed with it without the book self-destructing? What does this moral book tell us, if not that moral books are no good for moralizing, the first words are themselves stricken with the democratic insularity of the book, and only another writing can cure the book's illness, a writing that links men together by lines inscribed directly on the common earth?

One could say, following a time-worn formula, that the novelist Balzac and the moralist Balzac enter into contradiction here, and that this contradiction shows us how the literary matter, whether it wants to or not, is involved with the social matter. But that conclusion would be skimpy. This island that lies across the narrative indicates a more profound contradiction, a more essential link between politics and literature. This contradiction, or rather this connection stretched to the limit, is that of the link that ties literature to its condition, literarity. The function of moralist doctor and priestly gaze that Balzac assigns to himself are themselves possible only against the background of the new idea of "literature" that places novels in opposition to the islands of writing of literarity. Balzac's "morality" is not a matter of a reactionary prejudice that contradicts the autonomy of the literary work. It is this very autonomy that puts the writer in the paradoxical position of physician to the illness that gives rise to the work. "Literature" is that singular power that was founded on the ruin of belles lettres and old poetics, on the collapse of rules of representation that determined genres and modes of expression appropriate for one subject or another. Aristotle, Horace and their epigones had fixed these rules of representation to set up rules for the derangement of poetic fiction. But perhaps, in the place where the norms of poetic rules collapse, where the art of writing is reduced to the autonomous exercise of its own power, it encounters the other disorder, the more profound disharmony that literarity establishes between the occupations, the manners, and the attitudes of the community. The instant literature tries to make its absolute power the principle of a nobility or a new priesthood, it discovers the mutuality of this absolutist art and the democratic disorder of literarity. For whom, after all, is the new hero of literary aristocracy writing? Essentially for those men and women who *should not* read. The novel that tells of the unhappiness of the woman who read one single novel—and the most edifying of them all—seems to be in the new genre of the cheap newspaper serial.

But the link that connects the power of the novel with the misfortune of one who reads novels is an older matter. This absolutized literature thought of as Romanticism takes *Don Quixote* as its foundational narrative, the exemplary novel of a man driven mad by novels. We have seen that Don Quixote's madness is not taking fiction for reality. It is taking the book for truth, refusing the enclosure of fiction within an appropriate space. The book cannot be allowed to run free right and left, speaking "to those to whom it is suitable to speak and to those to whom it is not suitable." And literature itself is linked to this dis-connection [*dé-liaison*] of fiction, this madness of the island that becomes a world. We have also seen that Cervantes' book offers an exemplary division of this power of the book. The author leaves to his character the responsibility of the madness of the reader of books, and takes for himself the mastery that is its correlative.

From this original connection between the power of the writer and the character who is his hostage, we have seen two traditions emerge that define two ideas of literature. In the virtuoso tradition, the solidarity of the master and of the madman grants the former all the powers of the latter. Thus the figure of the magician-writer is formed who shows himself to us with his illusionist's paraphernalia, makes fun of his story and his characters, creates them and leaves them along the way, sends them on adventures or encloses them in a secret or enigmatic structure all the better hidden from the reader's shrewdness since it is actually only the secret of the nonexistence of the secret. That is the tradition that runs from Sterne to Borges, passing through Jean-Paul, Poe or certain stories by Henry James.

But there is also—and the fable of *The Village Priest* is an excellent illustration of it—the opposite movement, in which the writer confronts this relationship as a tension of literary mastery with its necessary and impossible condition, democratic literarity. To confront this solidarity between literary power and the banality or democratic *wandering* [*errance*] of the letter is to bring the writer's mastery to the point of rupture. Then it is the hostage who takes the master hostage, who draws him in and encloses him in the island of the book to the detriment of his own book, or who forces him to place his cause in the hands of those who care for the ills of writing and democracy: those engineers of souls who identify the network of material channels of communication and connecting with the new community, with the living book of the living law, the law of love.

But handing one's cause over to the engineers or "geographers" who write the meaning of the community on the soil is not, we have seen, a simple question of morality. It is also a question of poetics. The time of risky democracy, and of the utopias that try to order it, is also the time when literature, on the ruins of the old poetics, discovers its power to be as infinite as its solitude. With the old poetics of Aristotle, which based the power of writing on models, rules, or genres, this new poetics is contrasted, which wants to calibrate it on the power of the mind that is already writing itself into things, and must end by identifying itself with the very rhythm of the community. This power of the mind is already at work in nature, which writes its own history in the folds of rock or the grain of wood. It is at work in this life that doesn't stop writing itself, symbolizing itself, from its humblest steps, and that keeps lifting toward higher powers of writing and symbolization of itself. It is at work in this humanity whose language is already a living poem but that speaks—in the stones it shapes, the objects it makes and the lines it cuts into the land—a truer language than that of words. Truer because closer to the power by which life itself is written.

Literary solitude is born companioned by this new community of the poem with the movement of life. The encounter of literary power with democratic literarity is itself bounded by the proposition of a new writing of the new community: communal breath, lines of iron and water of the community animated by the living link, of the community as living work of art. The fixed gaze suspended over the island—we could, going beyond Balzac's thought, identify it with the suspense of literature between two possible fates. The first is the hand-to-hand combat of literature with that literarity that founds it and ruins it at the same time. It is the fate of the literary religion that finds its champion in Flaubert. This religion can assert the unconditional aristocracy of art only at the price of linking itself by fiction to the fate of ordinary lives seized by the madness of the letter: Madame Bovary, or Bouvard and Pécuchet. Its absolutized prose establishes itself as such only at the cost of confronting itself, differentiating itself, line by line, from the great prose of the world, "stupidity." This hand-to-hand combat of the fate of literature with the fate of its hostage ends by imprisoning the writer on the island of the book, at the copyist's table where ultimately he chains Bouvard and Pécuchet only at the cost of fastening himself to it as well.

The second fate is the marriage of literature with the new poetics, the one that is inscribed in the continuity that goes from the poem already inscribed in lines of stone or folds of earth to the communal symphony: breath of spirit, living work of art, poem identical with life. Literature is then identified with the poem of the community—its word accessible to all the senses, song of the people or rhythm of the Idea—codified to the point of canceling itself out at the time of the marriages of symbolist chorus to futurist machinery, until it ultimately identifies itself with the silent current of electricity or with the song of machines—in short, with the poem of the engineers of souls.

Balzac perhaps invents the first great figures of such engineers of souls with his Father Bonnet and Doctor Benassis. But he also experiences, not as ideologue but as novelist, the singular torsion they force the novel to undergo. In fact they do not remedy any "ailment" of the novel, they do not free the literary power from the literarity that gnaws it, except at the cost of dragging it toward another point of abolition. The fable of the engineer of souls makes the novel impossible even more than the fable of the island does. This *Village Priest* that is impossible to complete is the perfect example of those "badly designed" plots of the realist and psychological novel of the nineteenth century to which Borges contrasts the perfection of the plots of the moderns, from *The Turn of the Screw* to [Bioy Casares's] *Morel's Invention*. Certainly, the link between the detective logic of the story told and the logic of the fable that makes clear the motive of the crime is made of the coarsest thread, if we compare it to the science with which a contemporary of Balzac, Edgar Allan Poe, likens the writer's mastery in inventing clues to the cunning of the detective who deciphers them. In *The Village Priest*, the clues of the detective story, the priest's gaze, the novelist's logic and the moralist's intention chase vainly after one another, without being able to make the fable of the evil island and of the redeeming dam into one single book (having, as Aristotle said, its own magnitude and completeness) though they try to make the secret of the story into one single secret well hidden in the pattern of its carpet, or ingeniously deduced by the writer/inspector from the quite simple conditions of its fabrication. But perhaps it is precisely the badly organized tale, stretched between the logic of the narration and that of the fable, that leads us more surely toward the unique quality of literature, toward its secretless secret, which is none other than its interminable tossing between the democratic malady of writing and the utopia of hyper-writing.

So we can understand why Balzac keeps adding episodes along the route that leads his book toward the completion of its fable and the triumph of its morality. His political "backwardness" is for no other reason than his literary progress. And we could also meditate on the irony of the way this book reached its conclusion, the way this suspense between two literary destinies was settled in fact: in the form of the stupidest of stupid writings, a bailiff's notice.

# THREE

# Proust: War, Truth, Book

We know Proust's repeated protests: his book is the opposite of a chronicle of his life and his time: it is a construction, a fiction wholly oriented toward the demonstration of a truth that can be uttered only at the end. We also know that the final episode that makes this truth burst forth, the "*matinée* at the house of the Princesse de Guermantes*," was one of the first written by Proust. But *Le Temps retrouvé* [Time regained] comes to this revelation only after a long detour, devoted to an event that Proust obviously could not have foreseen in his initial plan, the war of 1914. How to explain this intrusion of the reality of war into the "dogmatic" plan of the work, which its author in 1914 boasted of having calculated exactly? No doubt Proust finds good reasons for this addition: if he introduced war episodes, he says to his publisher, it is as a natural prolonging of the lessons on strategy that the young officer Saint-Loup gave to the narrator visiting Doncières. The reality of this war would quite naturally come to verify these lessons. To these practical labors of strategy, though, a consideration that seems rather different is added. Monsieur de Charlus, he adds, will at the same time get something out of this Paris "teeming with soldiers like a city by Carpaccio" (1).

The terms of this explanation pose a problem, if not an enigma. They involve the necessity of confirming Saint-Loup's strategic theories measured against living reality. But the scenes introduced are not military scenes. There are to be sure some conversations on strategy, the paradox of which we will see further on. But mainly the book presents us with various extravagant scenes that culminate in the episode of the brothel, where soldiers on leave are occupied in providing pleasures to two aesthetes in love with virile beauty: the heroic officer Saint-Loup and the Germanophile Baron Charlus. The only soldiers we see are the ones supplied to us by this brothel.

How can we explain this gap between a declared objective and what it gives rise to, these phantasmagoric scenes of bombardments and this apotheosis or sadomasochistic apocalypse that seems to be less the beginning of *Time Regained* than an epilogue to *Sodome et Gomorrhe* [first translated as "Cities of the plain"], with [Bulwer-Lytton's] *The Last Days of Pompeii* somewhere in the background? How can we explain the other gap that accompanies it, between this sacrilegious representation of the nation's heroic soldiers and the unfailing patriotic orthodoxy declared by the narrator? The aesthetic question and the moral question converge in one single investigation of the true reason for the introduction of the war, and for the form the war episode takes. Apparently Proust had, through the episode with Albertine, led the games of truth and error to a point where the great peripeteia, the impact of truth, could intervene. And he had given himself the fictional pretext in order not to have to talk about it: the nursing home where he encloses his hero for many years. Why make him leave it on two separate occasions to include this war that can no longer contribute anything to the hero/narrator's path toward the truth? My hypothesis is this: if the war must be talked about, and talked about in that way, it is because this war that adds nothing to the truth of the book might indeed, on the contrary, take it away. For it carries within it the model of another truth antagonistic to that of the fictional demonstration. And it is this counter-fictional truth that must be refuted by the inclusion of war in the book. The inclusion of the reality of war in fiction is the inclusion in the book of another "truth of the book" that the book must settle. So much so that the mind chained to the "rock of matter" that the end of the episode speaks of is not just that of Charlus. It is also that of this war that Charlus disparages.

There is thus a very specific weaving of this other truth into the book's path of fictional truth. And in fact the war, foreign to the novel's design, seems to take in all the elements of its poetics. Just as Elstir's art transformed the land into sea and the sea into land, the mundane curfew transforms the great city into a village with tortuous streets, while the planes, on air raid nights, trace on the astronomic sky the constellations of idea according to the most Mallarméan logic. On another level, the war recapitulates the laws of the social world and those of the passion of love that the book illustrated, and makes them into the laws of national psyche. The war thus captures the elements of the truth of the book. But it is in order to rearrange them into the figure of another truth, from which the fictional truth of the novel must then be reconquered. The novel must wage its own war on war; it must wage a war of writing it.

## From Strategic Knowledge to the Truth of War

To grasp the principle of this, let's go back to those conversations at Don-cière about which the narrator, when he recalls them with Saint-Loup, tells us: "I was trying to reach a certain kind of truth there." What truth did these conversations bring out, then? "That the smallest events are only the sign of an idea that must be brought out and that often covers over others, as in a palimpsest." This phrase recalls the very program that *Time Regained* assigns the writer: to decipher impressions which are like the signs of so many ideas and laws. The strategy appears to be a variant, if not an example, of the science of signs that allows one to find ideas and laws in events, in arrangements of bodies. There is a military semiology that allows us to transform the confused narrative into a rational sequence, as any good physician does, but also to read a position on a plot of land as one reads a painting, by identifying its elements and the logic according to which they are present there, obedient to tradition, to texts, or some other necessity. The scholar of military semiology is not just a Clausewitz, he is also an Émile Mâle. This semiology thus seems like a fortunate science of decipher-ing the event. It is also an art superior to Elstir's, in which the pleasure taken in the game of appearances relies on an intellectual foundation, on a knowl-edge of laws. Finally it is a knowledge of truth and of lies that attains a for-tunate objectivity denied to knowledge acquired by amorous deception. This knowledge implements objective laws of the way in which bodies can dispose themselves to make other bodies suffer, in particular the laws of pre-tense. So it turns out to be superior to the knowledge the narrator acquires about Albertine's lies. No doubt he perceives in the lying woman's gaze gleams of mica that belie her discourse or divert its meaning. But these gleams that indicate distance from the truth do not indicate the direction toward it. The only "laws of love" are laws on the fashion in which one con-structs an object of love for oneself. They are laws of the necessary error that suffering alone reveals, which cannot be anticipated. There are, on the other hand, military laws on the production of lying and suffering. In Stendhal, the amorous and social strategy that Julien Sorel designed for himself in the image of Napoleonic strategy had as a counterpart Fabrice's incapacity to form a rational perception of what happened on the battlefield at Waterloo. The Napoleonic strategic model supported a lasting idea of a novel's character and plot. But it supported it through dissociation itself. The great theater of war, when it appeared, would swallow up in its non-meaning the calculated behavior of small-town strategists. Tolstoy had drawn an early lesson from it. He had rewritten the Napoleonic war by making the anarchy of love analogous to the anarchy of war. The narrator of *Du côté de Guermantes* [The Guermantes way] and *La Prisonnière* [The captive], for his part, seems to reverse things once again. He challenges the example of a novel's character-as-strategist, but he also notes the superiority of the calculations of military semiology over the vain deductions of amorous anarchy.

It is this superiority that war should brilliantly confirm. And that is what Saint-Loup asserts when confronted with the narrator's questions. But his demonstration is doubly suspect. Can one, the narrator asks, predict the length of the war? Certainly, Saint-Loup replies. It will be short. The sign of this is that the law of military planning did not predict relief of units. *In petto*, the narrator cannot prevent himself from adducing an entirely different interpretation: if the law did not predict the necessity to relieve units, perhaps it was quite stupidly because the strategists could not predict that the war might be long. Is the old Napoleonic feint still used in the modern total war? Certainly, the officer replies again: Hindenburg's maneuvers on the eastern front are pure Napoleon. This time, the narrator does not comment, but we can comment for him: Saint-Loup is speaking of the war the enemy is waging, the war it is waging on the Russian front. None of the consequences he draws from the strategic lessons at Doncières concern the war in which he himself is participating, the war the French are waging on the Germans. For this war of theirs seems to revoke the strategic example. Later on the narrator will say retrospectively to Gilberte that Saint-Loup was beginning to perceive this: "There is a side to the war that he was beginning, I think, to perceive, I told her, that is, that it is human, is lived like love and hate, could be told like a novel, and that, consequently, if such and such a person goes about repeating that strategy is a science, it doesn't help us at all to understand the war, since war is not strategic. The enemy does not know our plans any more than we know the goal pursued by the woman we love, and even our plans perhaps we ourselves do not know" (2). This paragraph revokes all the privilege of strategic science over amorous illusion. Strategy is perhaps a science, but it is not the rationality of war. This rationality is lived like love or hate. And it must be portrayed according to a logic of perception and passion. It must be portrayed as Elstir painted the sea, that is to say as it appears to us, as if it were the earth and as if the earth were the sea. It must be recounted as Dostoyevsky recounts a life: with characters who appear first as drunkards or scoundrels and who are revealed as beings of high spirituality and morality.

So the war reverses the truth of the semiology it was supposed to confirm. War is not strategic. It is no more legible than love. And one can write it only through this game of rectifications that undoes the illusions of a love projected on some passerby seen from a car. But the reversal of the semiological model doesn't stop there. The "Dostoyevskan" argument is presented here as retrospection. Yet it had in fact already been presented during the time of the war episode. Only it was neither the narrator nor Saint-Loup who presented it: it was Charlus the defeatist, the Germanophile. And the narrator had at the time thought him totally arbitrary. He did not see how Charlus could compare Dostoyevsky's ambiguous characters to the German enemy; "lies and ruses not do not suffice to make one assume a good heart that the Germans do not seem to have shown" (3).

The reasoning is strange: certainly the Germans' lies were not enough to prove their good hearts. But how does the narrator know they are lying? The answer to this question is even stranger: "During the time I believed what was said, I would have been tempted, when hearing Germany and then Bulgaria protest their peaceful intentions, to put faith in their words. But since life with Albertine and Françoise have habituated me to being suspicious of their thoughts, of plans that they did not express, I did not let any word, seemingly true, of Wilhelm II, of Ferdinand of Bulgaria, of Constantine of Greece, mislead my instinct, which guessed what each of them was plotting" (4).

On the ruins of strategic science a new, infallible interpretative skill arises. But this ability is quite singular, and the analogy that supports it quite lame. For the habit of encountering the lie was not able to create in the lover, while he was in love, an infallible instinct that would have allowed him to guess what the object of his love was "plotting." At the very most a rush of blood to Albertine's face or a sudden brilliance in her eyes had sometimes shown him the lie, without giving him the truth. And there was an utterly simple reason for that: for the lover to know this truth of the lie, the beloved—the liar—would have to know it herself. She would then be operating in the manner of the Napoleonic strategist who deploys the first ranks of combatants to conceal the fact that a large part of the troops has gone to battle elsewhere. But the anarchy of multiple individuals that make up the beloved/liar forbids her the rationality of this ruse. And the "lover's lie" is nothing other than anarchy itself, the fact that Albertine is a multiplicity of individuals who are looking for a multiplicity of other individuals. Thus there is no truth that can be deduced from this lie. On the contrary, the truth of a fact reported by Albertine can never be proven, except by its absence of a logical link, and the truth of her thinking remains indeterminable. So it is strange that the school of love could have taught the narrator an infallible knowledge about the truth of a lie.

But there is something even stranger in the comparison of the lover's experience to the experience of the war. For what the experience of love proved to the hero is that the beloved always lies to us, with a permanent lie that is not a characteristic trait but just the pocket change of the illusion objectified in the individuality of the beloved individual. Yet the political transposition of this experience of love is supposed to prove the opposite: the loved one never lies, the enemy always lies. In decent logic, Albertine's or Françoise's deceit should make the hero suspect first the words of the friend, the ally. It is Clemenceau or Poincaré he should suspect, or even the French press, before suspecting Wilhelm II or Ferdinand of Bulgaria. But the logic of war functions in a disjunctive way: first there is friend and enemy, and the same reasons, drawn from the same individual experience of love, make it that one cannot believe the enemy and one cannot not believe the friend. By separating friend from enemy, the war has also separated truth from lie. Love for Albertine made the hero incapable of untangling truth from the lie. On the other hand, love for the fatherland makes him incapable of mixing the idea of the fatherland with that of the lie, the idea of the enemy with that of truth. The possibility of calling into question this truth or this lie belongs only to those without a country, to the spectator Charlus. He alone can adhere to the philological mode of truth, can analyze the proposals of Brichot or Norpois to find signs in them of coherence or incoherence, compare the sayings of the French press with those of the German press and come to a conclusion on their equal probability of truth or falsity. The philologist establishes and puts into play protocols for examining statements. But, the narrator protests, the truth of statements is not a matter for philologists, but for protagonists. The truth of statement is not the correctness of the saying but the soul's power it gives to bodies in movement. That is the true lesson that Saint-Loup draws from *his* war and transmits to the narrator: "I am aware that words like 'they shall not pass' or 'we will get them' are not pleasant; for a long time they gave me as bad a toothache as '*poilu*' [French soldier of World War I—Trans.] and the rest, and no doubt it's annoying to construct an epic on terms that are worse than a grammatical error or an error in taste, that are that contradictory and atrocious thing, a vulgar affectation, a pretension [ . . . ] but if you saw all these people, especially the common people, the workers, the small businessmen, who didn't suspect the heroism they possessed within them [ . . . ] The epic is so beautiful that you would think, as I do, that words could do no more" (5).

## From Incarnate Truth to the Truth of the Book

Here Saint-Loup gives the narrator a lesson that is not just about politics but about poetics. In effect he teaches him that there are two kinds of epics. There is Aristotle's kind, where words must be noble. And the noblest of all words is the *xenikon*, the word that is foreign to everyday language. This Aristotelian poetics is also the Proustian poetics: style exists when there is the "foreign" element of metaphor that disappropriates the terms of common usage, de-idiomatizes them. War, however, ruins this style. Beneath the abolished epic of Aristotle it reveals another kind, an "idiotistic" [from *idiotisme*, meaning "idiom"—Trans.] or "idiomatic" epic in which what constitutes the value of an expression is its double appropriation: by the body that utters it, and by the act by which this body, by living out the phrase, accomplishes its truth. It is this epic that is expressed by the words "*poilu*" or "they won't get through." And the word "epic" is not just a metaphor to designate the heroism of the collective effort. The epic is a poetic genre. But it is a genre whose significance changed its meaning in Hegel's time. He is the one who defined the new, idiomatic nature of the epic. It is, he said, the Bible, the life story of a people. The epic is the becoming-flesh of the spirit of a people. It is the poem shaped in the certainty of a sentient identity that constitutes a people as people, in the appropriation of bodies, words, and deeds that weave a community, in the agreement between a way of being, a way of acting, and a way of speaking. This Hegelianism unites with a kind of Platonism: the most beautiful poem is the living community, where the idea has become the movement of bodies in common. And what takes over strategic knowledge (which is henceforth nothing but knowledge of the enemy) is this truth of the living poem, where the name is similar to the thing, the body similar to the name that describes it, where the vulgarity of "we will get them" and "they shall not pass" becomes the exact truth of their heroism and the result of this heroism: they did not pass.

So the "passionate" war is a strange passion, a passion that is wholly truth. It is the realization of a certain mode of truth: truth proven by transforming the pages of the book into living, suffering flesh, put to death and victorious from beyond the tomb. The truth of the patriotic epic is Christian truth, that of the incarnate spirit. Saint-Loup's war—whatever the illusions may be that he uses to mask his desire—is the "real" war, the unanimous war of all the cells that compose the individual-France, the war of the French of Saint-André-des-Champs, "lords, the bourgeois and serfs respectful of the lords or revolting against the lords": (6) two branches of one single family, that the war makes into two arrows converging toward the same border to defend it. The truth of the war is the identity-truth of the word made flesh. Saint-André-des-Champs is, as we remember, the typical "French" church, as opposed to Balbec, the "Persian" church, the church with the foreign name and the deceptive image, which we would imagine lashed by waves, whereas it is quite banally situated at a tramway junction, between a billiard parlor and a drugstore. Saint-André-des-Champs, on the other hand, is the church of a territoriality without metaphor and of a truth written in stone by an artist/man of the people, who sculpted on the porch the saints and chivalric kings, but also Aristotle and Virgil, of whom he had undoubtedly never read a line but whom he knew in another way, by a knowledge taken "not from books but from a living tradition at once ancient and direct, uninterrupted, oral, deformed, unrecognizable, alive,"(7) in short an Aristotle and a Virgil, entirely imaginary by the lights of academic criteria, entirely real according to a more profound truth: that of the spirit that living generations transmit. This truth that the medieval artist has carved in stone is the truth that still lives in the angelic way in which the sly little Théodore carefully raises Aunt Léonie's head; in the principles of '89 as imagined by Françoise; and even in the villainies of the plebeian Morel. It is this living truth, written in the stone, that comes down from the portico to become spirit incarnate, the living soul and actual poetry of the community.

Thus the illusion of the Persian church battered by waves is contrasted with the truth of the great human tide, flowing down from the portico of Saint-André-des-Champs to express the living soul of the stones. Charlus or Madame Verdurin can ridicule this Barrès-like style in articles by Norpois or Brichot. It is nonetheless the truth of the mind, the truth of what circulates between stone and flesh. It is the truth of France-as-protagonist or of the nation-as-individual from which the narrator, unlike the nation-less Charlus, cannot separate himself. He can only, he tells us, react like "one of the cells of the body of France," "a part of France-as-protagonist," just as, he adds, "in my quarrels with Albertine, my sad gaze or my stifled throat were a part of my selfhood passionately devoted to my cause" (8). Here again the analogy of love is devious. In reality the attachment of the hero to France-as-protagonist is the opposite of his attachment to the person of Albertine, and the opposite of what alone could appease the pain of her lies: the presence of Albertine and her cheeks offered as consolation for the lie that her words and looks betray. This suffering and this consolation were the very lure of individuation. On the other hand, to be a part of France-as-protagonist is to find the solution, in this instance economic, to what love for Albertine revealed: the irreconcilable multiplicity of individuals contained within what we call an individual, and whom we want to possess as such.

The war thus transforms into positive and indisputable truth what the entire novel has shown us as impossibility and as source of all suffering, the stubborn determination to want the individual to be embodied in people, to want the blind certainty of the human species to be transformed into a happy relationship of individual to individual. The narrator of *Du côté de chez Swann* [Swann's way] showed us this determination linked to an original privileged relationship: the mother's kiss, the point of certainty when human gestures become the fusional connection of a specific being to a specific being. And he showed us what this attachment signified, which is the original sin against literature: the letter written by the child to request the calming presence and kiss of the mother; the letter written to suppress the letter, to appease the unrest that the distance of writing constitutes. It is the same kiss the young man requests of Albertine, the sea goddess come from the waves on the Balbec beach, this kiss that is a substitute for the absence of an organ provided by the species for the communion of individual with individual.

The truth of the war is the truth—the counter-truth—of the mother, the anti-literary lure of fusional communion. What it puts into play will be illumined by another text: "Perhaps one believes it is lost, the genius of men who in the Middle Ages sculpted the Virgins of compassion, in memory of the sufferings of the mother of God at the foot of the Cross. But take this letter found in the compartment of a train carrying wounded soldiers. Take it, read it, and you will know that even if the barbarian invader destroys the masterpieces of Reims and our country churches, what will inspire them has not been exhausted. Beneath the breast of the women of France a treasure of piety subsists, and that same soul that our ancestors had summoned and set in the stone of cathedrals. We had become blind, but the oldest French beauty soars up from shadow and appears to us, and the great hours of battle, tocsin bells, victory bells, have revived us, have brought us back to living nature, to the truth of the depths of our race.

"Listen to what French mothers write to their sons. Not one, but all, each in her own way. It is a letter that slipped from the hands of a wounded soldier that we couldn't find [ . . . ] I have a taste for rare and precious papers that bring us closer to great minds. What wouldn't I give for a first edition of *Le Cid* or for a signed copy of *Esther*, dedicated by Racine to the young women of Saint-Cyr. But this letter from an illiterate woman, this stained elementary-school paper, surpasses the most sumptuous relics of art, and, having read it, reread it, copied it, I folded it up with a religious respect. I have just seen in the shadows the source from which the genius of our race has flowed for centuries" (9).

It is not Proust writing that, but Barrès. But shouldn't we begin to worry here about Flaubert's terror [of banality]: a tiny deviation, and I would be writing Paul de Kock. A tiny deviation on the theme of the mind come down from medieval sculptures into the living reality of mothers and children of France, and Proust would be writing Barrès: not just bad literature but anti-literature, the abdication of the truth of the book in favor of the truth of the anti-book, the maternal truth of the offered body that atones for the suffering of writing. It doesn't take much to bring together the initial scene of the kiss awaited and obtained with the first vision of the statues of Saint-André-des-Champs, and to draw from this origin a straight line that finishes in the national epic, in the book of living truth that the maternal earth carries, now turned into spirit of the communal poem. The novel, however, is the anti-epic. That it is, according to Hegel, the "epic" of bourgeois modernity must be precisely understood. The novel is not the new epic, it is the anti-epic. It completes the modern reign of the book that suspends the Christian truth of the book, the truth of the spirit that is made flesh in order to testify to the book. If the novel, and literature along with it, have taken Don Quixote as their hero, it is because his novel is precisely the defection of that truth, because his teaching is this: no body subjected to suffering and derision verifies the truth of any book. If literature exists as such, it exists from that knowledge, from the knowledge that the word is not made flesh. It exists, at the same time, from the invention of these quasi-bodies, from these fictional devices that construct their truth as the truth of this abandonment. The Augustinian "take, read" of Barrès is the path of this truth taken backwards. Through mothering fantasy, literature is led back to what denies it and what it denies, the truth of the book that is made spirit of flesh; the circle of the spirit that is offered as victim on the cross is made spirit of stone, spirit of the mother, spirit circulating between the mother's kiss, the patina of stones, and the fusion of them all in the collective epic. That is the "end of the book" that threatens the book: fictional truth replaced by incarnate truth; the triumph of the "spirit," this spirit that offers itself, through symbolism, as the truth of every work, against which the constructed fictional truth of Proust's work led a secret battle that the war transforms into an open war of truths.

That is where this brothel comes in, so little suited to illustrate some theory of strategy, this house of Jupien's where, for a few coins, the soldiers of the national epic serve the pleasures of the heroic Saint-Loup and the sadomasochistic rituals of the defeatist Charlus, until the whole business ends up in the catacombs of the metro, where miracle or sacrilege is realized: the direct fusion of bodies that no longer request any preliminary. With the sincere patriotic faith of the narrator, which is also that of Proust the individual, the fictional construction of the book contrasts the radical profanation, the spirit "nailed to the rock of pure matter." Truth made flesh in soldiers' bodies in the national epic then becomes a pure scenario of violence in a sadomasochistic system. This is not simply because the heroism of the struggle against the barbarians turns into the mercenary service of the villainous pleasures of a man without a country. It is above all the living truth of war that is returned to an illusory status: the illusion that the narrator described in *Swann's Way* about Mademoiselle Vinteuil. The sadist, he explained, is the artist of Evil, the one who exhausts himself in this specific lie which is to make Evil exist as such because, he believes, Evil alone gives pleasure.

In short, the profaning of national heroism is the profaning of the system of truth that heroism offered as triumph of the Mind and goal of the Book. The national sacrifice desecrated into a sadomasochistic lie is also the debased truth of the Christian body sacrificed to complete the truth of the Book of Life. And the episode of the catacombs and the primitive rituals to which they abandon themselves after leaving Jupien's house seems, like the second ending of the Gospel of John, added expressly for those who didn't get the point.

In Jupien's house Charlus is not the only one who receives some wounds of a somewhat different kind from those evoked by Barrésian lyricism. There is also Saint-Loup. The narrator does not describe to us the pleasures he takes in them. But we understand in any case that they must be the direct—or thought to be direct—satisfaction of desires that support this "passionate novel of homosexuals," which is what war is in the eyes of the narrator. This "passionate novel" is desire sublimated into a pure dream of medieval chivalry, virile friendship, chaste nights spent out in the open beside Senegalese soldiers, and heroic death inspiring a fanatical love in the men. Before Proust can unite Swann's way with the Guermantes' way in the Verdurin/Guermantes salon, the heroic Saint-Loup and the defeatist Charlus must be joined in the brothel. Why them, particularly? Because, now that Swann is dead, there remain these two representatives of what blocks fictional truth, the truth of art, that is to say the aesthetic lie, the lie of artistic truth, of art reduced to the true-to-life. These two figures must be annihilated. And it is this liquidation of aestheticism—rooted in the homosexual's lie about his desire—that the war episode must carry out. The episode in the Jupien house verifies the exact sameness of two seemingly contradictory forms of one single illusion. Its ritual verifies, over the body of Charlus and of Saint-Loup—who symbolically loses his cross there—that the truth of the patriotic body animated by the soul of the earth, of the mother and of stones, is strictly identical to the "passionate novel of homosexuals," and that both stem from the same original sin against literature, from the illusion that art is in life, that it is made to serve it and that life's purpose is to imitate art: illusion of the art-lover Swann who takes Vinteuil's sonata for "the national anthem" of his love, and finds in Odette's face the faces painted by Giorgione or Botticelli; illusion of the aristocrat Charlus who discovers poetry in the conversation and gestures of the socialite, or in the toilettes of Madame de Montmorency. Behind the living truth of the body animated by the collective soul, one must recognize this other "living truth," this other lie against art that one can call by the name that Baudelaire used for it, "dandyism." The heroic *poilu* and the socialite dandy, the sadistic artist of evil and the child greedy for the maternal kiss are all linked to the same lie. One must, then, chain up, that is to say link together but also to pillory, to nail to the rock of "pure matter," all these forms of "spirit," all these figures of truth/life [*vérité/vie*], that is of the lie against literature: the incarnation/sacrifice of the Word, son of God; the letter of the child who awaits his reward of a mother's kiss; the word of the dandy who sculpts his person and composes his life like works of art; the national epic of good-hearted soldiers. The "new" truth of war condenses all these truths, all these lies. The truth of fiction must chain together this chain of lying truths in the legibility of the narrative, build the span that links the beginning to the end, construct it against the final truth that war has come to offer. The novel of national energy offers itself as the truth of impressions of Combray, the truth of the France of Françoise and of the gardener, of the imps of the Roussainville donjon and of the angels of the portico of Saint-André-des-Champs. To annul this arch, to which the patriot Marcel Proust might easily consent, the writer Marcel Proust must construct another span, from the bed of the sufferings and pleasures of the child greedy for his mother's kiss to the bed of pleasure and pain of room 14B in the Jupien house.

It is then possible to glance again at the famous lines that open the episode of revelation in the courtyard of the Prince de Guermantes: "It is sometimes at the instant when everything seems lost to us that the warning arrives that can save us; one has knocked on all the doors that lead nowhere and the only one through which one can enter and which one has sought for in vain for a hundred years, one bumps against it without realizing it, and it opens" (10). The annoying thing about these doors that open without one wanting them to is that they can open just as easily at the first moment as at the last. This door of remembrance understood could have opened in the first pages of the book—the author already had his full catalogue of epiphanies—and, at the same time, there would not have been any book, any fictional demonstration of truth. The problem is not, then, to knock on all the doors so that chance can open Ali Baba's cave, the realm of ecstatic truth. The problem is to close, once and for all, the right door, the one that had to be closed so that "chance" can open the other one, the door of truth made flesh and blood. And that is the purpose those thousand and one war nights of rainbow explosives and sacrilegious orgies served. This war that the book's plan could not foresee became the occasion to confront literature with a total symbol of its negation, and thus to do what the novel might otherwise never have managed to do: to close the right door.

# PART III

# The Literature of the Philosophers

# ONE

# Althusser, Don Quixote, and the Stage of the Text

"In the history of human culture, our time is at the risk of appearing one day as being marked by the most dramatic and difficult ordeal there is, the discovery and training in the meaning of the 'simplest' actions of existence: seeing, listening, speaking, reading—the deeds that connect men to their works, and those other works that get stuck in their throats, which become their 'absences of works.'"

These lines, which outline the task of a generation, belong to the preface of *Reading "Capital."* And no doubt today's reader will specially perceive the intimate resonance of the dramatic relationship between the work and the absence of work and the dazzling haste of these great nocturnal texts by Althusser, written in one single draft as if to banish the night of the "absence of work" that is more banally called madness. But more than yesterday's project, or the symptom we could detect in it today, what interests me here is the way in which an idea of reading is formulated at the border separating the work from the absence of work. I will examine, then, the idea of reading that supports the Althusserian undertaking, the status it gives to the book and the theater of relationships between the text and what's outside, between writing and the politics it establishes.

Althusser's politics of reading gives itself a privileged adversary: the "religious myth of reading": the myth of the book in which truth is offered in its flesh in the form of an epiphany or parousia, in which the discourse written is the transparency of meaning in the obviousness of its presence, of meaning that offers itself as a person, and can be read at sight, without obscurity [*à livre et à ciel ouvert*: a combination of two common phrases—literally, 'open book and open sky'—Trans.]. The hero of this religious reading is Hegel, the one who sight-reads essence in existence, the glory of Easter—of spirit alive as a person—in the darkness of Good Friday. This religious/speculative myth of the immediate presence of meaning in the written is, for Althusser, what secretly supports the naive empiricism that identifies the words of the book with the concepts of science, and the concepts of science with objects we can hold in our hands.

There would be much to say on the somewhat too convenient way in which Althusser—and an entire generation along with him—constructed this rebuttal of religious reading, of a truth that forms and yields its meaning at sight. For even the book of the Christian religion can't so easily be reduced to the parousia of a body of truth. The body that accomplishes that return is the one that disappears between the descent from the cross and the discovery of the empty tomb. If there is a book, and if the book goes indefinitely back in its own tracks, tears itself apart between the verification of the Scriptures by incarnation and the verification of incarnation by the Scriptures, it is because the book always lacks presence. One never actually reads in it what Althusser sees in Hegel, "the unclouded sight-reading [*à ciel et à visage ouvert*] of the essence in existence." With the image of this book that is too easily open we can contrast that of the book as sky of which Saint Augustine tells us in the Thirteenth Book of his *Confessions*; this book never shows us anything but its dark side. The legible side is turned away, toward the side of the Father and the angels. So it is paradoxically turned toward the only ones who don't need to read the Book: the Father who is the origin of the word, and the angels who can read his decrees on the very face of the Father.

We can see, then, the advantage of this convenient identification of the religion of the Book with parousia in the Book: by coupling religious speculation with naive empiricism at the beginning, it ensures the entire chain of identifications whereby the economist and the humanist, the opportunist and the leftist, and all the other ill-matched couples symmetrically marked by the same original sin docilely take their places. The price of this convenience is to leave the door open to all kinds of singular "atheisms" that will make use of anti-myths generously borrowed from the other virtualities of the religious corpus and religious utterance—the summa theologica, negative theology, Pascalian wager, etc.—against the "religious myth of reading." Thus in Althusser identification allows one to validate *a contrario* and at little expense the curious figure of a parousia of absence, a way of reading in which absence is shown openly in presence.

The fixation on "religious myth" has an immediate effect: it ensures a certain mythification of the Book, it makes falsely obvious the book as unit, the book as thing, book as meaning. Let's read, for instance, this preliminary declaration of *Reading "Capital"*: "We must, one day, read *Capital* letter by letter—read the text itself in its entirety, the four Books, line after line. . . . " But to do that, we must first be assured that there indeed exists a book, *Capital*, that Marx wrote, and wrote in four Books. Does such a book exist? The authorized edition of the Dietz Verlag is not sure of that itself. The phrase *The Fourth Book of the Capital* only occurs in it as a rubric assigned in parentheses to the *Theories of Surplus Value*. And if this book exists, what is its last line? If I believe the same edition—and if I take away the *Beilagen* [appendices]—*Capital* ends with these words: "With that, we've finished with Jones." He's finished with Jones? But have we finished the Book? Doesn't Althusser's initial reference to the great Book leave us in a weird certainty about the book in general? This certainty about the unity of a continuum of writing, about its identity, will authorize a game ruled by displacements and metamorphoses, by shifts of meaning explicit or implicit, verified or unverified, between the book and the text, between the text and the work, between the voice of the text, the author of the book, and the subject of the work.

## From One Oversight to Another

Let us see this game at work, then, in the practice of Althusser reading Marx the reader of economists and especially in the theory of the "oversight" that the preface of *Reading "Capital"* places at the heart of symptomal reading. I will briefly summarize the analysis before pausing at a strange oversight by Althusser himself.

Althusser distinguishes two readings of classical economists in Marx. In the first, Marx reads Adam Smith through the model of Marx's own theory. He works out what his predecessor has seen or not seen, grasped or not grasped, the oversights he has committed, a failure to see what there was to be seen in the organization of capitalist production. The oversight then is only a failure to see what was present in the field of the visible since Marx himself saw it.

The second reading refers to an oversight immanent in the text of economists: no longer a failure to see what is in the field of visible objects, but a failure to see the concepts they themselves produced. By looking for the *price of labor*, and by identifying it with the value of the goods necessary for the subsistence and reproduction of the laborer, they had in fact found something else that they did not see because they weren't looking for it: the *value of labor power*.

The oversight, in this case, is no longer a matter of myopia, or an individual failing. It is a property itself of the field of the visible. The "value of labor power" and its complement, surplus value, are not just something that classical economy did not know how to see, but they define *its characteristic invisibility*, the impossibility or prohibition of seeing that are internal to the structure of its *seeing*. What it can see is an answer to its question, the "value of labor." What it in fact produces is the answer to another question, that of the value of labor power. It cannot see this answer since it answers a question that it did not ask, that the very structure of the field forbids it from posing to itself. This relationship produces a conflict in his text: "labor" is put there for something else, that it hides but that it lets us see that it hides, in the surreptitious change of subject that is at work between the value of *labor* and the necessary subsistence of the *laborer*.

The work of the second reading of Marx is, for Althusser, to make this invisible/visible seen, to produce the concept of it by producing the question that political economy did not know it was answering. This production of the latent text of classical economy is the production of a new concept, the production of a knowledge by occupation of the terrain over which economies had glided without knowing it. There is an essential relationship between the theory of reading and the theory of knowledge. A myopic reading corresponds to an empiricist theory of knowledge as sight, as sampling an object from the reality of vision. A symptomal reading corresponds to an idea of knowledge as production. Althusser theorizes elsewhere about this production as transformation of raw material with the help of instruments. Here, on the other hand, he analyzes it according to its etymology: *pro-ducere*, to lead forward, to make obvious what is latent. Thus Marx produces the concept of labor power by making obvious the blinding of classical economy with regard to what it produced with its tools—even if it means that he himself turns out to be unable to make obvious the concept of "producing" that he produces.

I would like to linger on one or two operations of reading by which Althusser makes possible this theory of "production," and on their implications. What, according to him, distinguishes the second reading of the economists by Marx is the way in which the "right" answer figures already in the text of the economists and figures there by pointing to the question that it lacks, in the form of a deliberate gap that can be marked by two parentheses enclosing a blank, which marks the place of the right question, of the missing concept: "The value of ( ) labor is equal to the value of subsistence goods necessary for the maintenance and reproduction of ( ) labor."

By making us see these blanks, Marx would have us see that the classical text itself tells us that it is keeping silent. Thus Althusser's demonstration implies a very specific usage of psychoanalytic theory. The restitution of a missing signifier is there identified with the "production of a knowledge": an event in science, an epistemological break. And for that, the relationship of the *seen* and of the *not-seen* must be specified as the relationship of an *answer* to a *non-question*, which is the non-question unique to "classical economics." The paradoxical desubjectification in the heart of which Althusser makes the relationship of the signifier to the subject function has a precise purpose: it makes the relationship of the obvious to the latent seem like the relationship of an answer to a non-question. It saturates the field of the *said* like a field of proliferating answers to questions still too rare. The field of knowledge is thus structured as a weaving of questions and answers that do not correspond to each other but whose very disparity is an earnest of sufficiency: an enormous reserve of answers to bad questions, waiting for good questions.

How is this structure constituted, and why should it be constituted? Althusser gives us the answer to this double question in the form of a singular oversight, a strange discrepancy between what he shows us in the layout of his text and what he tells us of this layout. Let's return to the sentence: "The value of ( ) labor is equal to the value of subsistence goods necessary for the maintenance and reproduction of ( ) labor." What we see are the blanks between the parentheses. But Althusser insistently designates them under another name: he calls them dotted lines. "By suppressing our dotted lines—our blanks—we merely reconstitute a sentence that, taken literally, designates in itself those places of emptiness, restores those dotted lines as so many sites of omission, produced by the fullness of the utterance itself."

This sentence is strange on two counts. How can one suppress dotted lines that one has not put there? And what is the reason they were not put there? I will answer for my part: if these dotted lines have not been presented, it is because they are not presentable. Dotted lines or ellipses, we know in fact to what genre of books they belong: elementary textbooks. In these books, the dotted lines are there for the missing words, words that the student must restore in a sentence left incomplete. These dotted lines that summon the right answer themselves assume the place of another procedure of knowledge: that of the answer to the teacher's question. They are there to verify that the student knows his lesson and knows how to apply what he has been taught. This is a pedagogical procedure that is more elegant than asking questions. The teacher puts the finishing touches to his work by disappearing into dotted lines. If he can disappear into them, of course, it is because he knows all the questions and all the answers. Thus he can absent the word, the word to be found that says that the pedagogue knows and that the student will know. Dotted lines are, strictly speaking, the presence of the teacher in his absence; they are the assurance that all the statements of the book are at once consistent and distributed in a complementarity of questions and answers, rules and applications.

That is what the "dotted lines" evoked designate: this structure of questions and answers simultaneously put into play and placed in absence. But it is this absenting that is redoubled, absented in its turn, when, in place of the dotted lines that still outline the teacher's silhouette, Althusser presents us with the virginity of white spaces protected by their parentheses. The parentheses are dotted lines denied, the twice denied figure of the teacher, who transforms the ordinary exercise of pedagogue into an extraordinary exercise of the scholar. In effect, what dotted lines ordinarily summon is simply a word: a word that the teacher knows and that the student has just learned, a word suitable for completing a certain sentence, whose meaning is exhausted in being made to leave room for these dotted lines. But what the white space between parentheses summons is something else, not any word at all, but a concept: the concept lacking in a statement to become scientific: in short, its lack or its own invisibility. If the quality of dotted lines is to indicate an absence, the quality of parentheses is to include, to mark a belonging. Parentheses include absence as belonging to the statement in which they function, as being its own absence. Parentheses appropriate the absence produced by suppressed dotted lines. They bring about, in other words, the parousia of absence. Their curve outlines the chalice of actual absence that gives the text its invisible quality, transforms the missing word into a missing concept, that is to say transforms, by means of lack, the word into concept. Thus the question/answer structure peculiar to the pedagogical exercise and community is transubstantiated into the question/answer structure peculiar to the scientific exercise and community.

What is this operation Althusser carries out on the signs of absence aiming for? To assure us that Marx did indeed create a science. But to do that, it has to identify the territory of writing with that of knowledge. It includes all that is written in a structure of knowledge, where it is question or answer, known or to be known. The disappearance of the teacher and his dotted lines in the blank space of the parenthesis insures, first of all, that one can answer questions that are not posed and, secondly, that there will never be anything else wrong but that. The defect of the text, and the wrong in general, are never anything but a displaced answer to a pending question. Ordinary progressive educational vision identifies the wrong with the question that has not yet found its answer. The inverted/denied pedagogical vision of Althusser sees the wrong, on the other hand, in the answer that has not yet found its question. The pending nature is never anything but the pending quality of the question—in the sense that a letter is pending—its yet-to-come quality. And this pending nature can always cease. Thus, in Marx, he tells us, if one looks carefully, one always finds elsewhere the questions—the right questions—to the answers to wrong questions.

What links the theory of reading to the theory of knowledge [*connaissance*] is a certain vision of the community of knowledge [*savoir*], a certainty that knowledge makes community. And this community is first of all that of the textual continuum, composed of answers and questions that are not matched, are still waiting to be matched. There is a seeming paradox in the Althusserian project: he wants to think in terms of a gap [*coupure*], a break. But symptomal reading thinks necessarily in terms of continuity: the way in which the "right" question nourishes the answer provoked by its absence. The necessary inclusion of "non-seeing" in "seeing" is conceived of in terms of an *episteme* à la Foucault. But the theme of the gap becomes completely paradoxical in this framework. The Althusserian gap is identified with the act that makes us see this non-seen thing that, before, had been the invisible inside of seeing. But exactly that is impossible in Foucault. From one *episteme* to the other, there is, for Foucault, neither any common question nor any common answer. The non-seen is only the excluded, the unthought only the unthinkable. This way of thinking of the *episteme* rules out unthought ever being in action, rules out answers to questions never asked.

In short, to think of Adam Smith's "non-seeing" in epistemic terms should logically rule it out from ever becoming Marx's seeing. Althusser wants to identify the production of the unthought with the change of *episteme*. But the very idea of *episteme* contradicts such an identification. Symp-

UNIVERSITY OF WINCHESTER
LIBRARY

tomal reading never encounters anything but inclusion, it always makes community, it always presupposes community. That is why the declaration of a gap in Althusser always takes the form of an act of violence. Thus, when it is a question of arguing the gap in Marx, we encounter a proliferation of arguments like "it's a fact" or "these are indisputable facts." That is because Althusser is perhaps less interested in the gap itself than in what gives rise to it—at the cost of making it, in the final analysis, unthinkable: the tightly woven fabric of right/wrong answers to asked/unasked questions, which is the space of science and of community: of community as place of knowledge, of science as power of community.

## The Desert and the Stage

To understand this fundamental concern, we have to make an apparent detour, by another story about answers, and a literary character who is also the unfortunate symbolic hero of all epistemical revolutions as well as of all revolutions in the means of production: the man who does battle with windmills, Don Quixote.

In chapter 25 of *Don Quixote* the hero goes into retreat in the Sierra Morena. He decides to be mad there, to copy the madness of his model, Roland, even up to the answer of a letter he has Sancho carry to Dulcinea. But the problem arises: on what should he write the letter? Since there is no suitable paper, Don Quixote writes the text in the book that came from the saddlebag of the madly-in-love Cardenio; he instructs Sancho to have it copied out at the first village by the schoolteacher or the priest. Sancho, though, raises an objection: how will he reproduce Don Quixote's signature? How can the letter be authenticated for Dulcinea's use? Don Quixote then reassures him through a series of irrefutable arguments: firstly, Dulcinea does not know Don Quixote's signature; secondly, Dulcinea does not know how to read; thirdly, Dulcinea does not know who Don Quixote is; fourthly, Dulcinea, or rather the peasant Aldonda Lorenço, does not herself know that she is Dulcinea. Sancho can thus depart fully reassured.

That way Don Quixote hangs his fate, the fate of his madness, on a letter that will not be read, on a letter addressed to an addressee who does not even know herself to be its addressee. To crown it all, the letter will not even be sent, since in a moment of distraction Don Quixote puts the book back in his pocket; this will not of course prevent Sancho from bringing back the

UNIVERSITY OF WINCHESTER
LIBRARY

answer to it. Through this absolutely failed act, Don Quixote carries out his duty, which is to be mad, to the end: his duty toward Dulcinea, toward the books of chivalry that he imitates, and, in the final analysis, toward the very book whose character, or rather hostage, he is. Thence, the solitude and madness of Don Quixote, the man who takes books literally, come to signify literature itself, the adventure of writing alone, of the body-less letter, addressed to someone who does not know that she—or he—is its addressee. They will signify it positively in the romantic theorization of the novel as modern epic. They will also signify it more prosaically in the eyes of philosophers of knowledge and of political realists, for whom "literature" signifies the unfortunate fate of language, the empty expression of the insanity of devotion, the law of the heart ridiculed by the law of the world.

Althusser's enterprise, however, is marked throughout by the dread of the Marxist intellectual, the dread of the intellectual fallen prey to politics: not to make "literature," not to address letters without addressee; not to be Don Quixote, the fine soul who fights against windmills; not to be alone, not to be the voice of one crying out in the wilderness, an activity by which one loses one's head, literally as well as figuratively. In the over-easy polemics against the parousia of the book, there is, much more deeply, more poignant, the dread of the fate of the Precursor, the one who preaches in the desert. "Communists, when they are Marxists, and Marxists, when they are Communists, never preach in the desert"—this was taught to the unfortunate John Lewis. Althusser adds, of course, that they are sometimes alone, and we know his words about Lenin, "the little man all alone in the plain of history." But one is precisely no longer alone as soon as there is a "plain of history," a place woven from its answers and its questions. Unfortunately the sentence that saves us from the desert—from the madness of solitary speech—is right away caught in a disjunction: "Communists, when they are Marxists, and Marxists, when they are Communists . . . " In the heart of this disjunction, there is not just the occasional risk that Communists might not be Marxists or Marxists Communists. There is a question of birth which is also a question of debt: that "imaginary debt" of which the preface of *For Marx* speaks, the debt of those who were not born proletarians. How can this political debt avoid becoming a literary debt, an infinite debt: the madness of speaking in the wilderness, of the letter without addressee written by Marxist intellectuals to Communist proletarians who do not know they are its addressees?

To avoid this solitude or this "literary" madness one must protect the communal cloth, the thick cloth of knowledge made of questions and answers that insures that in the final analysis, the questions asked by the "Marxists" are the right questions to which the "Communists" put up with being the orphan answers, one must protect the cloth against any tear, any dropped stitch. The question of science is first of all that of community. It is this community that must leave no place for a void of any kind, as the strange insistence of that other oversight, which denounces the "noble flags snapping in the void," bears witness to: the flags of the proletarian science of 1948—of Communists, not Marxists—or of the student protest of 1964, of Marxists, not Communists. The community of science is that of the cloth that leaves no void available to either one or the other group; of the cloth that guarantees against the risk of madness, *that is to say* of the solitude of the exalted soul.

This insurance of the community of knowledge against literary dereliction passes, in Althusser, by way of the mediation of this form-limit where literature emerges from itself, from this genre that sets politics in relationship with knowledge, the genre where one is assured of always speaking to at least one person: the theater. Faced with the Don-Quixotic risk, Althusser composes the text of questions and answers first of knowledge, then of philosophy, as a theatrical text. This composition is by way of a reflection on the theater that his 1962 article on "Le Piccolo, Bertolazzi, and Brecht" clarifies. What is at the heart of Althusser's analysis is the way in which the theater and the staging of a dramatic text make a connection with non-connection.

His demonstration uses Strehler's production of Bertolazzi's play, *El nost Milan*. This plays on the relationship of two seemingly disparate elements of the drama. On one hand, the play is a static representation of the Milanese sub-proletariat represented in its "natural" settings, a Luna Park, a soup kitchen, a homeless shelter. It's a series of silhouettes, of puppets passing each other, who with difficulty perform the same stereotypical actions in frozen time and who exchange half-audible derisory suggestions: beings who meet without meeting, forever separated from each other, separated from themselves in the immemorial time of the chronicle. The second element of the play, *the story*, turns up, as if by chance, at the end of each act: it is the story of young Nina whom a wicked young man, Togasso, is trying to possess, and over whom her old father watches. He watches so well that at the end of the second act he kills the one who threatened his daughter's honor. But, in the last act, when he comes, before going to prison, to say goodbye to his daughter, she rebels against his morality and decides to go against him, and leaves for the world of money and pleasure.

The question posed by Althusser is this: what relationship is there between the two elements of the play, between the time of the chronicle and that of the drama? And he answers: it is precisely the non-relationship that creates the relationship. What the production shows is this absence of a connection that makes sense. The sense of this little piece of drama on a corner of the stage at the tail end of each act is one of misunderstanding: the drama is the misunderstanding of the chronicle produced by the chronicle itself: the false conscience, the melodrama of the noble father who lives his existence and construes his condition in the faded finery of moral ideology. The illusory agitation of the drama is that of the "soliloquizing dialectics," the dialectics of the conscience, of the fine soul subject to the illusions of the law of the heart. This false dialectics is what must be destroyed in order to reach the true one, that of social relationships. That is what the girl does at the end of the play: she breaks the veil of illusion, she leaves the dialectics of conscience. She rejects the law of the father and goes through "the door that separates her from the daylight." She leaves for the true world, the world of money and prostitution, the one that produces poverty and imposes its conscience on her. She leaves, and we leave following her, with our conscience displaced for having been thus worked on by the demonstration of the relationship between relation and non-relation. We leave, new actors, actors of another kind, produced by the play, called to leave the dialectics of conscience in order to pursue the criticism at work in the play, to complete it in life.

Althusser thus produces a clear conceptualization of "non-relation": this is, and is nothing but, misunderstanding. He thus brings about a precise displacement. For the question of non-relation, its anguishing face, is first what is presented to us by that aphasic crowd that takes up the stage, that crowd where speech does not come through and produces nothing, that lives in an empty time, deprived of all direction. For the audience or the reader of 1962, this scene outlines a precise image: it is the asylum-world of the absence of work as presented in Foucault's recent *Histoire de la folie* [History of madness]. But also this anguish of speech that does not get through, of the story that doesn't manage to be written, of men whom neither speech nor time link as subject of a story, is an old anguish, an inaugural anguish that Marxism localized and exorcized in the concept of the lumpenproletariat. Despite the praiseworthy efforts made to give it an economic-social materialist genealogy, the lumpenproletariat is first of all a phantasmagoric name, a stage name, the theatrical embodiment of all the disasters of scholarly speech, the generic name of nonmeaning, of disconnection, of non-relation. This stage name fixes non-relation in place and denies it by giving it form in the system of social relationships. Expelled from reality, the no, the nothing of non-relationship then comes to be identified with the misunderstanding of social relationships. It becomes, under the term "ideology," a simple phenomenon of (false) conscience. Althusser thus repeats the initial attack of Marxism, the displacement of non-relation, its attribution to the ideological conscience: the conscience of the corner of the stage, that of the noble father, the derisory Don Quixote of high-sounding and empty words of morality and honor. The noble father is the pathetic puppet who must be isolated at his end of the act, on his corner of the stage, in order to say goodbye to him, and to go through the door to daylight.

Althusser's reflection on the theater thus defines a configuration of the stage and a localization of drama that serve to exorcise what the history of the theater has made so spectacular by dramatically tying together three terms: knowledge, father, and murder; which it has made blaze in the two tragedies that dominate theatrical history: in the Oedipal blinding of the desire for knowledge, this knowledge about which Tiresias had even warned that it was terrible since it brought no profit to the one who knows; and in Hamlet's vain quest for knowledge, and in particular, his vain attempt to use the theater to learn the truth about his father's murder. To this double figure the convenient character of the noble father/murderer responds, he who can be isolated on his corner of the stage where he reels off the tirade of ideology, the laughable discourse of a driveling father, half-Tiresias, half-Horatio. To this father one can bid farewell to pass to the other side, toward that "other side" of the theater whose direction the theater gives in negative, and toward which it arranges the exit, this other side that is called the real world. At the end of the play, reality is no longer the failure of speech, the failure of theory. It is the other side of the door that one opens while saying goodbye to the noble father, murderer, driveller.

To liquidate this father is also to liquidate the distress or madness of debt. By this theatrical strategy one can in fact buy back the debt, identify the movement of someone who "leaves"—who pays the debt of not having been born a proletarian—with the gift made to someone who was born proletarian and, by that very fact, lacks its theory—lacks the question to which he is the answer. For the movement by which the Marxist becomes Communist to be identical to the movement by which the Communist becomes Marxist, the space that separates the solitude of writing from the solitude of the aphasic crowd had to be made into a tightly woven cloth of questions and answers. For that, literature had to be led to that theatrical limit where non-relation is once and for all liquidated, where reality wins with one blow by killing ideology. Althusser grasped the technique of the theater, of a certain theater, as the heart of Marxist dynamics. Starting from that he creates a double dramatization: he dramatizes the text of theory as interlocution, and the relationship of theory to reality as the relationship of the play to its denouement.

## The Theater of the Text and its Exit

The theatrical impulse is, then, not just the necessary passage to stage the scene of the community of knowledge. It also determines the dramaturgy unique to the philosophical text. Althusser in fact produces an extraordinary theatricalization of the text. First of all it's a practice of interlocution, of set-ting the stage and assignment of roles. Thus the "political economy" and the "classic text" in Althusser come to see, write, and speak in place of the writer Adam Smith. Later on the Althusserian text will be invaded by the prolifer-ating horde of subjects with initials, combining Beckettian rarefaction with Brechtian pedagogism: M.L. victoriously responding to John Lewis, AIE, PP1 and PP2, the element 1 and the element 2 of PSS . . . Not simply use-ful abbreviations but personified concepts, concepts that speak. That con-cepts speak instead of subjects, that is the first characteristic of the inter-locution specific to the Althusserian text.

This use of initials for the interlocutors corresponds to the placing of their speech between quotation marks. Quotation marks are both dialogic indica-tors and ontological indicators. At the same time that they portray interlocu-tors, they define the substance of their speech. On one hand they introduce quotations. But these can be speaking subjects or non-speaking subjects. They are often semi-quotations, substances of quotations that tell the thought of the other without reproducing his speech, or by changing his identity. These unincorporated and reincorporated words then come to en-counter the notions that the use of the same quotation marks functions to place in suspense or suspicion: questioned concepts, challenged for what they claim to designate, or ideas advanced on certain conditions, indices or place-holders that mark the place of the true concepts that they are not yet. A whole drama of quotation marks thus oscillates between a twofold function: that of outlining the opposing camps, and that of insuring the continuum of questions and answers that give scope and meaning to the opposition. Interlocution is always at the same time that of struggle and that of liaison. Always it poses relation as including non-relation and excluding the void.

This drama of initials and quotation marks gives oddity to the page of an Althusser script—grimoire surcharged with indicators of reality, stage directions, overlaid with quotation marks and parentheses that displace the statements, their modality and the identity of the speakers, that give consistency to or remove it from voices, italics that withdraw words from ordinary usage and couch them in the direction of their meaning. Althusserian typography proliferates to surround nonmeaning and reduce it to its corner of a page. This work on the letter exorcises the Don-Quixotic madness, it saturates the page with relationships of community and conflict. This typography thus becomes the obvious mark of a typology in the dramatic sense but also in the religious sense. It establishes a drama of incarnation that makes the intelocutors of the book's page exist together in the real world: classes and class struggles, Marxism-Leninism, the worker's movement and others.

Althusser's work is significantly involved with the question of the real. In *For Marx* he accuses himself of having yielded, because of his indebtedness, to the empiricist and moralist sirens of the "end of philosophy" and of this "passage to the real world," proclaimed by *The German Ideology* and particularly necessary for intellectuals breaking with the bourgeoisie. In *Reading "Capital"* he insists on the radical separation between the process of thought and the process of reality, between the concrete of reality and the concrete of thought. But this farewell to the naiveties of realism does not settle the question, for it avoids the heart of the problem. The heart of the problem for Althusser is not to keep the real separate from thought, but to save it from nonsense, withdrawn from the reality of errancy, of disconnectedness and madness: the reality of Don Quixote, of literature or of the lumpenproletariat. This reality of literary madness, before any polemics on the relationships of thought with reality, must be replaced by another reality: one produced by the theater as *its* exit: the exit door to daylight produced by the dramaturgy of relation and non-relation, by the staging of interlocution, isolating in its corner of the stage and dismissing in the correct manner the dialectician of conscience or the moralist of *praxis*. The drama of the text aims to preserve this reality which is open only as the last outcome from closure itself, on the stage of the drama, of everything that comes out.

This identification of reality as the theater's only way out has two remarkable consequences. The first is expressed in Althusser's negative reaction to all "practitioners" of exiting, to those who want to leave too soon, by the wrong exit, when the time hasn't come. He wants to prevent any exit from the stage before the denouement, and also to keep people from coming onstage at the wrong time, people we're supposed to meet only at the denouement. Cordoning off the (wrong) exits is the condition for theater to use the logic that can open the right one. That is the second consequence: symptomal reading becomes a movement that closes the ways out to liberate at last the only way out, the encounter with reality. Exemplary, in this regard, is the reading of Rousseau practiced in the text of *Cahiers pour l'analyse* [Journal for analysis]. Analysis is deployed here from "gap" [*décalage*] to "gap," from closing of exit to closing of exit, to the point where Rousseau is surrounded, convinced of having encountered the reality of the class struggle and dodging it by fleeing ahead of time into his misreading, fleeing into ideology: the nostalgic ideology of small-scale, property-owning artisans incapable of facing up to capitalist ownership.

Assuredly this "reality" teaches us more about Althusser than about Rousseau. For the formulation of the terms of relationship between individual property and political community in Rousseau has much more to do with the tradition of Plato and Aristotle than with the grandeurs and decadences of small-scale artisanal ownership. The materialist "explanation" is in fact a signpost of an exit, the proof, by evasion itself, that the exit is indeed at the end, when the "dialectics of conscience" has reeled off its last tirade. The only problem is obviously that the exit is never put to the test, except by the infinite evasion of someone confronting it.

But reality, in Althusser, also takes on another face, that of the history of the "worker's movement" and its atrocities. In the preface of *Reading "Capital"* there is a strange passage where, after having spoken of reading the classic texts of Marxism and of the theoretical conditions that had made us capable of reading them, Althusser continues on, not about texts, but about *works* [*oeuvres*] that the method must one day make legible: "The same is true for the 'reading' of works still theoretically opaque on the history of the worker's movement as the 'cult of personality' or the very grave conflict that is our present drama: this 'reading' will perhaps one day be possible on con dition that we have identified correctly what in rational works of Marxism can give us the resource to produce concepts indispensable to understanding the reasons for this unreason [*déraison*]."

It is worth pausing on this declaration, which might seem merely topical (1). For, at the price of a change of status of the Marxist text that becomes a *work* and thus holds out its hand to its sister, the "irrational" or "opaque" work, to draw it into the fabric of "works of knowledge," and at the cost of introducing a new subject, an author of works between quotation marks, the history of the worker's movement, the theory of reading inverts what it has just advanced—the critique of the great Book—and what it will establish— the separation of the actual process from the thought process. At the point where theory encounters politics, it reintroduces what it had initially rejected: a great Book of reality, a great book of history. The essence cannot perhaps be read there in existence. But nightmares, as well as hopes, are read in it as works, still obscure but bound to be legible when their sisters, the "rational works," have asked the questions to which they are the answers that have come too soon. A Stalinist concentration camp or a Vietnamese resistance group are some works awaiting questions that will allow them to be read, but are already caught in the common fabric of knowledge. And the same is true for all those thirty years of the Stalin system sheltered under a concept between quotation marks, "the cult of personality," the euphemism sanctioned by the Communist Party of the Soviet Union, euphemized in its turn by the quotation marks that suspend it and reserve it. The concept between quotation marks is something like an umbrella under an umbrella, the euphemism suspended and at the same time placed in the space of its knowledge: a common space, even exemplarily common: common to the Communists—and to the masses for whom they affect to speak—and to the Marxists who, by quotation marks, give it the status of an answer without a question, awaiting the identification of its question; a space common to the innumerable masses of what is called the international worker's movement and to the scientific community. Between the rational works of Marxism and its irrational works the canvas is stretched. The quotation marks are the mark of science, of the little science necessary and sufficient to conjure away all the horror and all the nonsense. What is essential is that there be, in the texts of theory as well as in the reality to which theory gives rise or confronts, only works, never absence of works, never madness. The essential thing is that history never be mad, that we never find ourselves alone with this tale of sound and fury told by an idiot, that we never call out in the wilderness.

There is, in the heart of the Althusserian moment, something of which it is difficult to speak but that is nonetheless central: a thought of madness, a rigorous connection established between the madness of history and an intellectual's risk of madness. The presupposition of the Althusserian enterprise can be expressed this way: to tear history away from its madness, the intellectual must first of all guard himself from the risk of his own madness: the Don Quixotic risk, of the law of the heart, of the battle against windmills, of sending letters without addressee. In order not to be mad, in order not to be alone, he must establish himself in solidarity with all *works*, in the community of science and the worker's movement. He must refuse to produce, by the hastes or delays of the law of the heart, the least void or the least tear. Althusser has thus chosen a certain struggle against madness, the struggle against a *certain* idea of madness. He has chosen solidarity with all "opaque" works, a solidarity without quotation marks, as the condition of their legibility and their redemption. He has identified absolute evil as the solitude of the absence of the work. For the intellectual as well as for history, everything was worth more than the absence of the work.

For all that, we know that he did not prevent solitude, madness and night from closing in on him. Certainly it is futile to say that he lost his wager, and to conclude from that that it must have been stupid. It is worth the trouble, on the other hand, just to keep our eyes on him: to keep our eyes open to what the desire to make history reasonable leads to, to what is implied by the fear of speaking in the wilderness, the fear of the letter without addressee.

Maybe it really is better to write without addressee. And maybe, rather than still seeking to make the legacy productive, the concepts that Althusser has left to us to work on, maybe it is better to restore to his text the solitude—and I don't mean oblivion—to which it has a right, to restore the status that he vainly sought to win from the letter without addressee. I would like, for my part, for us today to let his voice reach us as the voice of a poet reaches us, a poet who died, probably mad, in one of those obscure works of the "history of the worker's movement," a camp near Vladivostok, Osip Mandelstam:

> *Forever remember my speech for its taste of unhappiness and smoke.*

# Deleuze, Bartleby, and the Literary Formula

One of Deleuze's last texts is called "Bartleby or the Formula" (1). This title is a good summary of his unique way of reading. Remote from any tradition of the sacred text, he instead describes the work as the development of a formula: a material operation that the materiality of a text produces. This term, "formula," situates the work's thinking in a dual opposition. On one hand, the formula is opposed to the story, to the Aristotelian plot. On the other, it is opposed to the symbol, to the idea of a meaning hidden behind the narrative. Thus *Bartleby* is not the story of the quirks and misfortunes of a poor clerk. Nor is it a symbol for the human condition. It is a formula, a performance.

We will see, however, that the clarity of principle of this dual opposition does not so easily survive its application. And the purity of the "formula," in its analytical detail, is subject to more than a to-and-fro between the opposing poles of story and symbol. But the case of *Bartleby* seems privileged. In it, the formula of the book is in fact summed up in the materiality of a linguistic formula: the famous *I would prefer not to* with which the strange clerk challenges his employer's most reasonable and courteous requests. The formula, in one sense, is only this block of words, this pure mechanism that forms the essence of the comic. And *Bartleby*, Deleuze tells us, is a comic story, to be taken in the most literal sense.

Only the comedy of the formula is not just something mechanical tacked onto something alive. It is the mechanical that disorganizes life, a particular life. The formula erodes the attorney's reasonable organization of work and life. It shatters not just the hierarchies of a world but also what supports them: the connections between the causes and effects we expect from that world, between the behaviors and motives we attribute to them and the means we have to modify them. The formula leads the causal order of the world that rules what we'll call, in Schopenhaurian terms, the world of representation, to its catastrophe.

Bartleby's formula thus achieves in five words a program that could summarize the very notion of literary originality. And its very utterance is strangely close to the ones that define this originality. "To prefer not to" can be paraphrased and interpreted in different ways, one of which is: "to renounce preferring," "to want not to prefer." In this version, it becomes formally equivalent to one of the canonic formulas that regulate the will of literature—I mean the famous Flaubertian principle: there are no beautiful or ugly subjects, no reasons to prefer Constantinople—the splendors of the Orient and of History—to Yvetot—the dampness and history-less dullness of the French hinterland. There aren't any because style is an absolute way of seeing things (2).

We know the formula but without recognizing its exact range or the uniquely metaphysical nature of its implications. It declares the rupture of literature as such from the system of representation, of Aristotelian origin, which upheld the edifice of belles-lettres. The heart of the system was the principle of the normative power [*normativité*] of what is represented. According to this principle, it was the subject represented that ruled the forms of its representation, the appropriate genres, and also the corresponding modes of expression. According to whether one represented kings or burgers, shepherds or animals, one had to choose poetic forms belonging to different genres and implying different laws of composition. Different languages and tones had to be employed: from the noble unity of the tragic style where the maidservant expresses her low thoughts in the elevated style of her mistress to the picturesque diversity of the novel where each person speaks the language that matches his social status.

In brief, what upheld the mimetic edifice was the hierarchy of the represented. And it is just this that the Flaubertian formula ruins. The simple abolition of this hierarchy signals literary rupture, the collapse of an entire normative system and of all the criteria of recognition of the validity of the works attached to it. The question is then posed: what actually supports the edifice of literature, and what provides the measure of the worth of its works?

There is a kind of easy and widely vouched for answer. It consists in saying: where there is no longer an external law, there is an inner law. Literature replaces the verifications of mimetic resemblance and the norms of *inventio*, of *dispositio* and of *elocutio*, by the demonstration of its own power. Its truth is *index sui*. This idea of literary autonomy and self-demonstration is itself interpreted in three ways. First version: the power of the work is the power of the unique individuality that produces it. Second version: it is the power of the totality self-contained and generating its own rule of unity. Third version: it is the pure power of language, when it turns away from its representational and communicative uses to turn toward its own being.

All these answers look good, and have had long successful careers. But they remain, to use Mallarmé's expression, "witticisms of the stage and of prologues" [*plaisanteries de tréteaux et de préfaciers*] unless they provide themselves, more or less discreetly, with an entirely different foundation (3). We have known since Saint Paul that the autonomy of one freed from the old law is his enslavement to the power that has ransomed him. What supports the "autonomous" work of emancipated literature is a heteronomy of another kind, it is its identification with a unique power of thought, with a specific mode of presence of thought in matter that is also heteronomy of thought.

All the projects that have tried to give consistency to literature have relied, more or less explicitly, on one single metaphysics. They have sought to replace what gave poetic *tekhnê* its foundation, or that *physis* whose work *tekhnê* imitated and completed. They have demanded, as foundation of literary thought, a different nature, counter-nature, or anti-nature, that is to the *style* of literature what *physis* was to the art of representation.

Style, I will recall here, according to Flaubert, is an *absolute* way of seeing things. Words have a meaning, even when they are used by writers. And *absolute* means *released, set free* [*délié*]. Style is the power of presentation of a released nature. Released from what? From forms of presentation of phenomena and from the connections between phenomena that define the world of representation. For literature to assert its own power, it is not enough for it to abandon the norms and hierarchies of *mimesis*. It must abandon the metaphysics of representation and the "nature" on which it is founded: its modes of presentation of individuals and the connections between individuals; its modes of causality and inference; in short its entire system of signification.

The power of literature must then be sought in that zone before representative sequences, where other modes of presentation, individuation, and connection operate. It is exactly this exploration in which the young Flaubert engages in that first *Tentation de saint Antoine* [Temptation of Saint Anthony], which gives his declarations on literary absoluteness the essential base, without which they would only be theatrical witticisms. That is the content of the "temptation" to which Anthony is subjected by a devil who is to begin with a Spinozist, but in the manner of the nineteenth century—a Spinoza as contemporary with Schopenhauer. After Anthony's encounter with a proliferation of monsters—of bodies without organs—this devil drags him on an aerial journey through spaces where Anthony hears pieces of his being crashing together with shrill screeching and lingering shudders. This movement of dissociation of the body from the world of representation leads Anthony toward the discovery of strange new forms of individuation, which the devil enumerates as "inanimate existences, inert things that seem animal, vegetative souls, statues that dream and landscapes that think" (4). These forms constitute, he tells him, a "chain without tip or end," that one can grasp neither by the beginning nor by the end, but at the very most by the middle.

The unique power of literature finds its source in that zone of indeterminacy where former individuations are undone, where the eternal dance of atoms composes new figures and intensities every moment. The old power of representation stemmed from the capacity of the organized mind to animate a formless external material. The new power of literature takes hold, on the other hand, just where the mind becomes disorganized, where its world splits, where thought bursts into atoms that are in unity with atoms of matter. That is what the pedagogy of the Spinozist devil explains to Anthony: "Often, because of anything at all, a drop of water, a shell, a strand of hair, you have stopped short, eyes fixed, your heart open.

"The object you were contemplating seemed to encroach upon you, as you bent toward it, and ties were formed: you clutched each other, you touched each other by subtle, innumerable embraces" (5).

These subtle embraces, these landscapes that think or these thoughts-as-pebbles—it would not be difficult to translate them into the Deleuzian lexicon. A more modern devil would translate them into those commands uttered in *Mille plateaux* [Thousand plateaus]: "To reduce oneself to an abstract line, a stroke, to find one's zone of indiscernability with other lines and thus to enter haecceity as one would the impersonality of the creator" (6).

But the problem is not to show that Flaubert was thinking like Deleuze before he existed or that Deleuze continues the vein of *The Temptation of Saint Anthony*. Flaubert's text is taken here as an illustrated version exemplary of the metaphysics that literature requires to exist as a specific art, as a specific mode of the immanence of thought in matter. What is opposed to the laws of *mimesis* is the law of this world underneath, this molecular world, un-determined, un-individualized, before representation, before the principle of reason. What is opposed to *mimesis* is, in Deleuzian terms, becomings and haecceities. It is the emancipation of expressive details, the entrance into a zone of indeterminacy, the discovery of fraternity. Flaubert expresses things in the pantheist lexicon of Romantic times. He gives a standard Romantic version of metaphysics that literature requires for its "autonomy" to have a meaning. Proust or Blanchot will both criticize the coarseness of Flaubertian metaphysics and of the poetics it implies. They will give more sophisticated versions of each. But fundamentally there is only one metaphysics of literature: the metaphysics of Maya's veil torn off, the wall of representation pierced to the groundless ground [*fond sans fond*], the place where thought discovers its power is identical with the power of matter, where the conscious equals the unconscious, where the *logos* is revealed as *pathos* and *pathos*, in the final analysis, as *apatheia*. It is this metaphysical nucleus of literature that this line of *Antigone* reinvented by Hölderlin illustrates, the line where Antigone speaks of the fate of Niobe changed into stone:

> I know that like the desert she has become.

The translator's treason [*trahison de traducteur*] effected by Hölderlin is exemplary of the passage from one signifying system to another. In fact the Niobe of Sophocles and mythology survived the metamorphosis permitted to the laws of the world of representation. According to a simple mimetic principle, the grief-stricken mother became a rock wet with tears of despair. On the other hand, the Niobe of Hölderlin, the Niobe of the era of literature, leaves the signifying system of *mimesis*. She becomes a desert, a rocky expanse where figure and meaning are abolished, where *pathos* is equal to the apathy of inert matter.

There is a metaphysics of literature. Let's call it the metaphysics of un-sensed sensation [*sensation insensible*]. Only this metaphysics, which grounds literature, also establishes it in the infinite contradiction of auton-omy and heteronomy. How can one wish for the abolition of the conscious in the unconscious? This metaphysical aporia is transposed into a problem of poetics: how to link together in the form of the work the emancipated atoms of thought-matter? The claim of literature seems to enroll it right away in the evil infinite denounced by Hegel, in the *symbolist* distance between the abstract idea of the new work and the dispersion of epiphanic moments. The fine Flaubertian idea of the book that "would all by itself hold together by the internal force of its style" (7) is torn between a global idea of the *inventio* of the book and the singular power of atoms of unsensed sensation that the power of *elocutio* carries with it. And the terms of classical poetics then re-arise: what *dispositio* of the book can make the first agree with the second, or, to adopt Flaubertian terms, can string a necklace from those "pearls" that *Saint Anthony* supplied loose (8)? The solution, practiced by *Madame Bovary*, has general value: it consists of accompanying the representative molar scheme, its procedures of identification and its narrative sequences, by the molecular power of emancipated expressive details. That is to say, it consists of reinserting these details into the mimetic circle. By way of example, Flaubert constructs a consistent plan made of percepts, feelings and tempi. He hollows out classical narration to transform a love story into blocks of percepts and affects untangled. What is he doing, for instance, in the scene in *Madame Bovary* where Charles meets the young Emma at the farm where he comes to take care of her father? Flaubert makes the molecular power of the thought turned pebble equal the descriptive power of a detail: thus the description of that melted snowdrop falling, in sunlight, on the watered silk of Emma's umbrella. The power of emancipated expressive details makes each episode, as well as a moment of narration, a metonymy of the beautiful totality of the work. Thus classical narrative unity is confirmed and reinforced by the power of the void that becomes the atmosphere common to each and every one of its atoms. Let's agree to call *impressionist* this poetics that reconstitutes the universe of representation with atoms of anti-representation. This poetics makes imperceptible the power of the imperceptible. Literature is produced by making itself invisible, by combining the molecular music of affects and free percepts with the molar schemes of representation. The literary power of style thus becomes, in the final analysis, identical with the art of the Aristotelian mimetician, who had to know how to hide himself in his work. Here it is literature itself that hides its labor by accomplishing it, that makes indifferent the difference that results from the principle of indifference, from the principle of non-preference.

Flaubert's example can help us understand the steady meaning of Deleuze's operation on literature, which seeks to bring literature back to its essential rupture from the world of representation. Works of literature constantly betray the purity of rupture. Constantly they distance themselves from the logic of sensation that grounds them; they reinsert freed expressive details into the mimetic universe in two ways: by making them atmospheric features, and by arranging them in the beautiful totality of the work conceived on the Platonic and Aristotelian model of the "smoothly functioning organism." Deleuze's analyses aim always to unmake this compromise or this contradiction. But the inconsistency of literature is also the consequence of the philosophical ground—Romantic, idealist, German—on which it has been conceived. And Deleuze's intervention aims at the same time at tearing from this ground the literary logic of sensation, so as to establish it in another territory where Burke, William James, or Whitehead take the place, more or less discreetly, of Hegel, Schelling, or Schopenhauer. To represent this thought in imagistic terms, it is a matter of substituting a vegetable metaphor of the work in place of the idealistic alliance of mineral atom and animal organism (9).

This work animates Deleuze's interminable confrontation with Proust's work. The case of Proust in effect represents the highest contradiction in the enterprise of literature. Proust laid bare the conjuring trick characteristic of Flaubert's impressionist poetics and the effect of a "moving sidewalk" that results from it (10). Instead of it, he demands a greater philosophical honesty, translated in a poetics that gives greater force to metaphor. We know even so that he does not resolve the contradiction of the autonomous work founded on the heteronomous logic of sensation, except by a play on words about the book "printed in us." The world of representation's moments of fracture do not make a book, and epiphanies must be linked together in a plot of awareness in the Aristotelian manner, producing truth without knowledge of the subject who bears it. It is in this Aristotelian *muthos* that the disruptive logic of *pathos* yields its power. The logic of the "beautiful animal" or of the well-constructed work thus takes literary rupture back into itself. And Deleuze's entire effort is to expel the animal/mineral metaphor from Proust's work to construct a coherent figure of the Proustian *antilogos*, a coherent figure of the vegetative work as manifestation of an *anti-physis* for which Charlus's body, surcharged with signs, serves as blazon. We know that Deleuze must, in order to construct this unique logic of *antilogos*, return three times to Proust's text. We also know that the *antiphysis* thus systemized bears a name, that of schizophrenia, or, more simply, of madness (11). What is ultimately opposed to the work-organism or cathedral is the work-spider's web, the thread of the schizophrenic narrator stretched between the paranoia of Charlus and the erotomania of Albertine. Ultimately, the neatness of the metaphysics of literature and of the contradictions of its poetics tends to give it a coherence that strictly assimilates literary space and clinical space.

But the work is not madness. And Deleuze's difficulty in giving a coherent counter-model of Proustian dissociation explains the privilege he assigns in his analyses to forms that do not pose the problem of synthesis of the heterogeneous, of short works like the short story or the tale, characterized by the unity of the fable. Deleuze also privileges specific kinds of fables: narratives about metamorphoses, passages onto the other side, about becoming-indiscernible, formulaic narratives, narratives that are processes, that relate unusual achievements; narratives centered on a character subject to metamorphoses, or on a performer of metamorphoses or indeterminacies. In short he privileges narratives that reveal, in their fable, what literature performs in its own work.

The purity of the distinction that contrasts the formula to the story on one hand and to the symbol on the other then becomes confused. The Deleuzian "formula" tears the story away from the world of representation only by deporting both more or less explicitly to the symbolic. Bartleby's performance, like that of the singer Josephine, in Kafka's story, or that of Gregor Samsa in *The Metamorphosis*, always shows at the same time what the performance of literature consists in: the power of indeterminacy or metamorphoses. We must, then, correct Deleuze's initial assertion: Bartleby's formula, like Gregor's transformation, is indeed literal, and at the same time it is not so. The tale is, from this point of view, a privileged structure. It is the magic formula that tells the story of a magic formula, that metamorphoses every story of metamorphosis into a demonstration of its metamorphic power. Thus Deleuze's analysis institutes a rather peculiar play between what was classically called the form and content of the work. He tells us that literature is a material power that produces material bodies. But, most often, he demonstrates this to us by telling us not what the language or form effect, but what fable tells us. He insists on the idea, borrowed from Proust, that the writer creates, in his mother tongue, a foreign language whose effect entrains all of language and makes it swing over to its outer limits, which is silence or music. But how does he illustrate this? By evoking the "painful squeaking" of the voice of Gregor metamorphosed. Or, in Melville's *Pierre, or, The Ambiguities*, by the character of Isabelle who "affects the language of an incomprehensible murmuring, like a basso continuo that bears all of language in the chords and sounds of its guitar" (12). But Kafka's language gives us only the transcription of the words that Gregor emits, and an observation about the strangeness of timbre he experiences. The "painful squeaking" creates no other language in language. The same is true for the incomprehensible murmuring or the basso continuo of Isabelle. In vain does the text say she cannot speak, in vain it speaks to us of the sounds of its guitar, it is in no way affected by this silence or this basso continuo.

But we can discern where this comes from, this basso continuo that we hear no more than Deleuze does in Melville's smooth text: from Schopenhauer's pages on music. By invoking problematic differences in language and by likening the operation of the text to what he tells us, Deleuze in fact subsumes literature under the concept of music: not as a particular art, but as a philosophical concept and an idea of art; this music that, in Schopenhauer, directly expresses the music of the real world, of the a-signifying and undifferentiated world that resides beneath schemes of representation. In brief, the analysis of the literary *formula* sends us back to the givens of the *story*, to givens that function as a symbol of the power unique to literature. The oppositions by which Deleuze defines the unique quality of literature turn out, then, to be unstable. To challenge all reintegration of molecular revolution into the schemes of representation, and end the contradiction between autonomy and heteronomy, he asserts a performative conception of literature, but by doing so he returns it to the logic Hegel designated as symbolism. Faced with a literature that annuls its principle by accomplishing it, Deleuze chooses an exemplary literature and an exemplary discourse on literature: a discourse in which literature shows its power, at the risk of showing only fable or allegory, a discourse where one can show it in the process of performing its work. But showing that operation most often signifies, in Deleuze, focusing the analysis on the figure of an operator. That means accepting anew the oppositions of Aristotelian poetics, centering the literary text on *character* to the detriment of *action*, to make the character the driving force behind the fable.

In fact it is important to be attentive to what could pass as an inconsistency in Deleuze. He descants on the virtue of molecular multiplicities and haecceities, of non-personal forms of individuation. He goes on about the individuality of an hour that dreams, or a landscape that sees. But his analyses always come to center on the "hero" of a story. More than the appearance of marine creatures on the Balbec beach, it is Charlus's posturing that interests him. He tells us that great works of literature are patchworks, yet in the incredible mosaic, textual and human, of *Moby Dick*, Deleuze's attention is fixed on Ahab alone, the character par excellence, the monomaniac governed by the single thought of confrontation with the great white wall of the sperm whale. Bartleby's case is just as significant. Bartleby in Melville is a character without a face, summarized in the five words of his formula. In Deleuze's analysis, though, he comes to join the gallery of exemplary beings among Ahab, Prince Myshkin, and Christ.

How can we explain this seeming return to a poetics of the story and its "hero"? To do so, we must take into account the relationship between poetics and politics. And here again the Flaubertian counter-example can be illuminating. The Flaubertian machine, at first sight, fulfills the task set by Deleuze well: to saturate each atom. And yet Flaubert, by annulling character, by privileging haecceities and by saturating each instant of the story with the movement of molecules, finally gives the narration back its privileged status. It seems, then, that the molecular revolution of literature returns, in other terms, to the old Aristotelian alternative, the choice between privileging action or character. Flaubert chooses haecceities over characters and the law of the *cogito*. But by doing this, he sacrifices the *becomings* [*les devenirs*] to the story. Deleuze, however, makes the opposite choice. By privileging the anti-narrative power of becomings, he concentrates power in the exemplary character, who becomes the operator of becomings and the emblem of becoming. The analysis of the literary character and his formula connects with the analysis of the figure in *Logique de la sensation* [Logic of sensation]. The pictorial logic of sensation isolated the *figure* by taking traits of character away from it, by preventing it from forming a continuous story in a community with other figures. But it also held back on the imagistic level, it crucified that figure so ready to escape into psychotic indeterminacy. The text on Bartleby offers a literary equivalent of the pictorial figure, the Christ-like figure of the *eccentric* [*l'original*]. Deleuze borrows from Melville's *Confidence Man* the notion of the eccentric as the character/point of view that projects a specific light on the fable. He also borrows from it the idea that a novel cannot include more than one eccentric. But the conceptual treatment he devotes to this figure of the eccentric conspicuously exceeds Melville's suggestions and intentions. The eccentric becomes in Deleuze a figure of a new kind. He resembles the pictorial figure by dint of his solitude, which blocks the unfolding of narrative logic, and also by virtue of his ability to symbolize the very movement of the work, that of a schizophrenia confined to the actual composition of the text. But even more than the pictorial figure, he is given the power to condense, as in a coat of arms, all the qualities of the work. He manifests "flamboyant traits of expression" that mark, Deleuze tells us, "the obstinacy of an imageless thought, an answerless question, a logic without rationality" (13). Similarly, Eccentrics inherit the famous power of the writer, that of creating another language within language. Their words are, Deleuze tells us, "vestiges or projections of an original language, unique, primal." They "carry language to the limit of silence and music." That is because they are in our nature "witnesses of a primal nature," revealing at the same time the "masquerade" of our world (14).

We can make two observations here. First of all, the power of Eccentrics is strictly identical with the power of the writer, that of style as "absolute way of seeing things." Deleuze wants to see this power of de-liaison that is itself untied [*déliée*] released into novelistic haecceities embodied in a character. But we must also note the role they play in denouncing the masquerade of our world. The Deleuzian will no doubt be surprised by the clearly negative nature that this game of masks and simulacra assumes, that Deleuze had previously contrasted positively with the Platonic idea. But the Schopenhauerian will find himself on familiar ground. In the opposition of an essential music of primal nature to our world of masquerade, he will recognize the opposition of will and representation. And the eccentric is an exemplary figure of the fate of will en route toward its annihilation, under two opposing forms. On one hand, he is the will exacerbated, carried to the maximum point where it is broken. It is, in Ahab, the excessive will that abandons itself: thus Bartleby, by embodying the stubbornness of not preferring, heralds the great conversion of will into a nullity of will [*néant de volonté*]. But the eccentric, the inimitable character who does not imitate, is also the peculiarity opposed to the mimetic dyad of model and copy or, which comes to the same thing, to the father/son dyad of filiation. The literary power of the eccentric is precisely the one that Schopenhauer confers on Music, direct expression of the real world sustained beneath the world of representation. The novel's eccentric gives his musical principle to the "figure" that undoes pictorial figuration. He manifests the power of the work as an encounter of the heterogeneous, that is to say not simply as the unpredictable composition of impersonal multiplicities but purely as an encounter between two worlds.

Here surely lies the heart of the Deleuzian difficulty. To the dualistic and vertical world of model and copy he seems at first to oppose a horizontal world of multiplicities. To the contradictory work, torn between the materialism of the thought-as-pebble and the idealism of the beautiful animal or of the symmetrical building, he seems to oppose the unique plan of this *patchwork* [English in original—Trans.]. To the model of filiation, its imitations and its culpabilities, he seems to contrast the fertilization of the plant by the bee, all vegetable and schizophrenic innocence. And yet this simple opposition of two images of the world is immediately thwarted. It is not the dissolution of the figure in the colorful impasto that the exemplary painting brings about, but its crucifixion, its establishment at the center of a contradictory impulse where it signifies the contradictory work of pictorial de-figuration. And the same is true for literary text: instead of filling up with the disorder of haecceities, it centers itself imperiously on the heroic figure of the eccentric who reveals its actual meaning. Deleuze, I've been saying, wants to substitute one ground for another, an empiricist English ground for a German idealist ground. But these seemingly surprising returns of a crudely Schopenhaueran metaphysics and of a frankly symbolist reading of texts show that something comes to thwart this simple substitution; in place of the vegetable innocence of multiplicities it imposes a new figure of struggle between two worlds, conducted by exemplary characters.

It is not a question here, of course, of inconsistency. To understand the seeming contradictions of Deleuzian poetics, one must reestablish the order of mediations that gives literature its political function. The population of the novel is also the promise of a people to come. This political stake is inscribed in the very project of literature, in the principle of non-preference. The equal value of every subject, the reduction of all hierarchies of representation to the great egalitarian power of becoming, involves a relationship of literature to equality. But which, exactly? What relationship does the molecular equality that grounds literary innovation have with one that the political community can actualize? It is Flaubert again who gives the classic formulation of the problem. For him political equality belongs to the order of illusion, of the representative *doxa*, incapable of changing levels, of reaching another account of unities. It is not the human individual who is the atom of equality. That is what his famous letter to Louise Colet says: "Devil take me if I don't feel just as kindly toward the lice biting a beggar as I do toward the beggar. I am certain moreover that men are no more brothers to each other than the leaves in the woods are alike: they worry together, that's all. Aren't we made with the emanations of the universe? [ . . . ] Sometimes after looking at a pebble, an animal, a painting, I feel I have entered it. Communications between humans are no more intense" (15).

This is the politics inherent to the metaphysics of literature. This politics leads from the equality of human individuals in society to a greater equality that only reigns below, at the molecular level—an ontological equality that is truer, more profound than the equality demanded by the poor and the workers. Behind the masquerade of fraternity there is the sympathy that links together the fibers of the universe. Or there is, in Schopenhauerian terms, compassion, which is the affect unique to the writer since it exceeds the order of relations between human individuals (16). The community of brothers has no ontological consistency, no privilege over the old community of fathers.

It is this antifraternal equality that Deleuze rejects. The people literature invents cannot be reduced to the population of local affections of universal substance. The molecular revolution is indeed a principle of fraternity. But it is not by its direct plot development that molecular equality accomplishes what is unique to literature, and establishes its fraternity. The great invention of literature, free indirect discourse, must be snatched from Flaubertian quietism. It is not the equality of subjects in the writer's eyes that it establishes, but the suppression of fictional privilege. Free indirect discourse does not express the absolute point of view of style; it manifests the actual opposite of representation, which is not the indifferent music of atoms, but fabulation as the "becoming of the actual character when he himself sets about to 'make fiction [*fictionner*],' when he enters into the 'flagrante delicto of legending [*légender*],' and thus contributes to the invention of his people" (17). The molecular revolution leads not to the equality of the daughter of Père Rouault and the daughter of Hamilcar before the omnipotence of the writer, but to the power of *fictioning* that the farmers of the Ile aux Coudres use when, at the instigation of the filmmaker Pierre Perrault, they "revive" their legendary dolphin-fishing, contributing thus to establishing "the free indirect discourse of Quebec, a speech with two heads, with a thousand heads" (18). The seeming contradictions of Deleuzian discourse, the privilege given to the mythical character, are thus cleared up: it is the fabulating character who is, after all is said and done, the *telos* of anti-representation. "Fabulation" is the true opposite of fiction. It is the identity of "form" and "content," of the inventions of

art and the powers of life. You will have noted that it is with reference to another art, cinema, that Deleuze develops this notion most clearly. The forms
of what was called, by an ambiguous term, "cinéma-vérité" lend themselves
ideally to this transfer of the power of art to the fabulating/fabled people.
Compared with this *telos*, literature then takes on the function of mediator.
It goes into combat against the powers of representation as powers of the Father. The seemingly contradictory focusing of Deleuzian analysis on the
"hero" is, in fact, a focusing on the mythic combat from which must come a
shared fabulation, and a new fraternal people. The stories privileged by
Deleuze are not just allegories of the literary operation, but myths of the great
combat, of the fraternal community that is won in the combat against the paternal community. Eccentrics are not just embodiments of literary production, they are mythic characters who destroy the community of fathers, the
world of models and copies. They thus make the power of "the other world"
effective as the power that destroys this world. Crazy monomaniacs like Ahab
carry the figure of the father who wants and prefers to the point of self-de-
stroying excess. Beings without will, like Bartleby or Billy Budd, annihilate
the figure of filial obedience by a similar excess. They transfix it by identifying it with a radical non-preference. The tragedy of eccentrics thus liberates,
in rather Hegelian dialectics and a discreetly Wagnerian dramaturgy, the possibility of the man without qualities who is also the fabulator, the lying man,
the man in possession of the powers of the false, the last of which is called
truth. By destroying the portrayal of the father, which is the heart of the representative system, it opens the future of a fraternal humanity. As such it effects a passage similar to the Christian passage of the old to the new
covenant. "Bartleby is not the sick man, but the doctor of a sick America, the
new Christ or the brother of us all" (19).

Deleuze sees this fraternal future beginning in another fiction by
Melville, *Pierre, or The Ambiguities*, the story of the fraternal and incestuous
union of Pierre, the legitimate son of the dead man, and Isabelle, the illegit-
imate daughter. Of course, we could evoke Wagner again in passing, but also
the Hegelian analysis of *Antigone* in which the brother-sister couple seems to
be the true core of the family as spiritual power. And the entire text on
Bartleby could be read as a free and displaced commentary from Hegel's
pages on Greek tragedy. But the important thing is not to portray again the
German and Greek shadows that Deleuze's "American" scenario suppresses.
It is to see how this scenario combines two stories: a story of original sin or

original rupture with regard to the paternal order, and a story of an innocent fraternal world, wholly ignorant of that order.

In fact there is, in "Bartleby or the Formula," the presentation of an American utopia that might be—that could have been—the other image of the great fraternal hope: the society of comrades in contrast to the world of proletarians; another great hope, also confiscated, but still rich in possibilities, counter to the Soviet utopia, which from the outset was devoured by the paternal figure. The American revolution did not just break with the English father but also perverted his very power, to actualize a society without fathers or sons, a small nation of brothers on the road together, without beginning or end. It founded a minority America whose novel has that power of minority languages, or of minorities in language, uttered by Kafka, the German Jew from Prague. Deleuze outlines the philosophy of this fraternal America: another metaphysics of literature that is constructed around the James brothers, Henry the novelist and William the philosopher. Supposing that this America exists, we can wonder what makes Melville its prophet. But this choice of Deleuze has nothing approximate about it: the incestuous novel of Pierre and Isabelle—if we forget the family massacre that concludes it in Melville—in fact represents the exact point of encounter between two contradictory founding fictions: a dramaturgy of the dead father and of original sin; and a myth of the autochthonous, a dramaturgy of brothers and sisters walking about in a world that has never had a father. It is possible to see how this conjunction of opposites arises from the book that plays, in Deleuze's analysis, the role of guide, sometimes avowed, sometimes tacit. I mean the *Studies in Classic American Literature* by D. H. Lawrence.

The aim of Lawrence's book is to extract from American literature the true secret of a new world still shrouded in twofold mists: the dream of purity of an idealism still enclosed in the European and Christian universe of the father and of sin; and then the dream of freedom of an innocent and fraternal democracy. The two authors who complete the cycle, Melville and Whitman, in a way symbolize these two dreams. Melville embodies the man bent on the cross of the Ideal, on board the ship of maniacs of the Idea, hunting the being of blood and instinct, and crushed by it. Whitman embodies the unanimist dream, the democracy of naked souls who walk along the highway, with no aim but to travel, with no other form of society than one born in the ability to recognize oneself along the way.

But we feel, reading Lawrence's pages, a tension that seems to go against the explicit teleology that they argue: a derision that is mixed into his recognition of the greatness of Whitman, the pagan; a secret complicity with regard to Melville, the Christian. He sees in Whitman the messenger of the future, but he notes in him a twofold limit: on one hand his love for his fellows still encloses *sympathy*, the power of feeling-with, in the old idealistic charity; on the other hand he has the naiveté of an immediate realization of a fraternity that has gotten rid of evil and sin. Melville, though, the man who confronts the monster, seems the bearer of a superior artistic power, which is also to say of a superior power of truth. The American truth that Lawrence wants to expose amounts to a Whitman who has internalized Melville's reasons, restored to democratic *sympathy* the idealistic power of wrestling with the Angel and with the beast.

That is, in one sense, what Deleuze tells us by summoning up a fraternal America from the mortal struggle of Ahab or Claggart, who would have made the "mask of the father" fall and allowed the reconciliation of the Eccentrics—the men of "primal nature"—with ordinary humanity. But Deleuze seems to resolve the tension by reversing Lawrence's logic. He gives Melville the reasons of Whitman. He transforms Bartleby, the voluntary recluse, into a hero of the American open road. He makes the Pierre-Isabelle pair the initiators of the society of friends, and he makes Melville the representative of this America that from the start wanted to be like an anarchist community. We can readily imagine the irony of a Lawrence confronting the picture of this America. Here again Deleuze seeks to establish a coherence of literature, a coherence of the people it invents. It is a question of displaying in literary rupture the radical rupture with the society of fathers that the world of representation really is. But everything happens as if this coherence, built by force, immediately grew confused. Deleuze sings of the great highway of souls set free. But how can we not be struck by the image he comes to offer of this world "in process, an archipelago," which is that of fraternal individuals: "A wall of loose, uncemented stones, where every element has a value in itself but also in relation to others" (20)? I think this is one of the last of the great, strong images that Deleuze has left us. It is also one of the strangest. We understand that "loose [*libres*], uncemented" stones conflict with the architectural layout of communities founded on the law of the Father. But in a text whose Messianic connotation is so marked, certainly more so than in any other, why does the image of the whole in motion that must guide the explorers on the great road have to be the image of a wall? It is no longer the innocence of vegetable proliferation that is contrasted with architectural order, or with the disposition of the elegant animal. It is a loose [*délié*] wall, an oxymoronic figure that wants to evade opposition, but that perhaps presents us, at the same time, with the ultimate figure of contradiction inherent to the aesthetic mode of thinking, to the union of autonomy and heteronomy that is at its heart. But this figure also seems to block the mediating function of literature, to bar the road of shared fabulation, that of the people to come. And, no doubt, there is, in Deleuze, something like an interminable postponement or deferral of the promised fraternity. He undertakes a never-ending autocorrection, an infinite rectification of the image of thinking that he offers. As if he always had to separate "nomadic" thinking from that universal mobilism [*mobilisme*] to which it is so easily likened. For universal mobilism is also a quietism, an indifferentism. Literature has shown that in its texts, and the *doxa* that rules today gives us caricatures to illustrate it. At the time when the dominant discourse bases order on the assertion that everything is always moving everywhere with a movement that no one should disturb, Deleuze attacks this *doxa* "against the grain." He stops us before this strange wall of loose stones, whose problem is not how they hold together—a problem of equilibrium solved through the ages—but how their assembly becomes the norm, and represents the world of fraternal liberty.

But the paradox of this loose wall does not, for me, mark merely the need to differentiate nomadic thought from its caricatures. It seems to me also to represent the aporia of the passage that Deleuze summoned literature to clear by piercing, once and for all, the wall of the world of representation, by inventing a fraternal political people building from the type of individuals and from the mode of equality of individuals that his ontology defined, from the very mode of existence of the manifold that it establishes. And the question "What is this wall of loose stones?" sends us back to the question "Who is Deleuze's Bartleby?" What is this brother-Christ who frees us from the law of the father? This strange Christ, instead of being the Incarnation of the Word, comes from the office of *dead letters*, where he has seen only the limbo of letters without addressee, or rather addressed to an absent addressee, a Father-God who has no hands to open any letters, no eyes to read them, no mouth to speak; a deaf, mute, blind father, who sends his son Bartleby into the world only in the manner of a wall that bounces a ball back, to make him utter and "incarnate" one single phrase, namely that he, the "good" father, the schizophrenic father, prefers nothing. For he has no organ to choose anything, since his organs, his mouth, his eyes, his hands, are dislocated everywhere, in every place and every time of the world, and because he is in fact nothing other than their dislocation.

The problem, as we have seen, is that from this substitution of the psychotic father for the father of the Law, no other fraternity is normally formed, only atoms and groups of atoms, accidents and their incessant modifications. Nothing else is formed except the identity of the infinite power of difference and the indifference of the Infinite. And the question remains: how can one make a difference in the political community with this indifference? Difference must be made by an intercessor, by the Christ-like figure of the one who returns, "eyes turned red," from the other side, from the place of justice, from the desert, and has nothing to say except indifference. This intercessor must then perform not one but two operations. He must oppose the old law of the fathers with the great anarchy of Being, the justice of the desert. But he must also convert this justice into another, make this anarchy the principle of a world of justice conceived on the Platonic model: a world where human multiplicities are ordered according to their deserts.

Deleuze's Bartleby, this brother-Christ, messenger of a schizophrenic father, can then be recognized as the brother of another literary character invented by another philosopher who asked himself the same question, with the help of the same Christian reference. I am speaking, of course, of Nietzsche's Zarathustra. What Deleuze charges Bartleby with is exactly what Nietzsche charged Zarathustra with, messenger of Dionysus, Christ or Antichrist, charged with announcing one single truth, with knowing not that God is dead—news that interests only the last of men—but that he is mad. From this truth of the radical "non-preference" of God—this God who could also be called Becoming, Being or Substance—it is a question of forming the principle of a new justice, which is called "hierarchy," a name that Nietzsche writes and comments on abundantly in the margins of *Zarathustra* but that Zarathustra himself never utters, for, to utter it, one must first be the mouth capable of uttering the equality of difference and indifference—or the Eternal Return—and of forming listeners capable of hearing it, capable of laughing with Zarathustra's laughter, without transforming it into its travesty, the "donkey festival." The future of "justice" in Zarathustra's message goes through the necessity of cutting this link, which is at the same time impossible to cut, between the aesthetic education of "superior men" by Zarathustra and the comedy they make of it: the "festival of donkeys," or perhaps, quite simply, "Nietzscheism." And the aporia of the passage between ontology and politics is marked, in the book's conception, by the irresolution of the problem of its ending. There is the planned and unwritten ending that would have shown us a Zarathustra as legislator, establishing hierarchy. There is the end of the book published in 1884, the closing of the seven seals of the "Fifth Gospel." And there is this fourth book, privately printed in forty copies, which reopens the sealed book by portraying the "Nietzschean" comedy put on by "superior men."

It is indeed a mission parallel to Zarathustra's, a mission of clearing the way between ontology and politics, which Deleuze entrusts to literature in general and to Bartleby in particular. And it is true that Deleuzian justice is called, at the furthest extension of the Nietzschean "hierarchy," fraternity. It is a question, then, of clearing the path between the egalitarian desert justice of the mad God and the justice of a fraternal humanity. And that affair, Deleuze tells us, must be thought of as comic. Literature is the comedy that, given the great laughter of the mad God, clears the way for the fraternity of men on the road. But this comedy, like that of *Zarathustra*, is twofold. Under the mask of Bartleby, Deleuze opens to us the open road of comrades, the great drunkenness of joyous multitudes freed from the law of the Father, the path of a certain "Deleuzism" that is perhaps only the "festival of donkeys" of Deleuze's thinking. But this road leads us to contradiction: the wall of loose stones, the wall of non-passage. We do not go on, from the multitudinous incantation of Being (21), toward any political justice. Literature opens no passage to a Deleuzian politics. There is no Dionysian politics. And this wall, as free as its stones may be, is one before which the joyous expansion of the philosopher-children of Dionysus comes to a stop. Revenge, perhaps, of the old Euripides, so reviled by Nietzsche. He had indeed foreseen the philosophers: Dionysus does not want any philosopher disciples. He does not love philosophers, only donkeys. Revenge, too, of Christ on Dionysus. The brother remains Christ or Bartleby, figure of the intercessor, if not of the crucified one. And this wall of loose stones is like those multicolored rainbows, like those aerial bridges that Zarathustra had to cast toward the future, at the risk of seeing them resemble the counterfeits that enchanters and fools made of them. But, of course, the strength of every strong thought is also its ability to arrange its aporia itself, the point where it can no longer pass. And that is indeed what Deleuze does here when, in one single gesture, he clears the way of Deleuzism and sends it into the wall.

## Sources

"From Wordsworth to Mandelstam: The Transports of Liberty" first appeared in J. Rancière ed., *La politique des poètes*, Bibliothèque du Collège international de philosophie, Paris: Albin Michel, 1992.

"Rimbaud: Voices and Bodies" appeared in a preliminary form in *Le Millénaire Rimbaud*, Paris: Belin, 1993.

"The Body of the Letter: Bible, Epic, Novel" borrows some themes from the volume *Politicas da escrita*, Rio de Janeiro: Editora 34, 1995.

"Balzac and the Island of the Book" was first published in Number 5 of *Villa Gillet*, November 1996.

"Proust: War, Truth, Book" takes some themes from the text "Du côté de Saint-André-des-Champs," published in Number 1 of *L'Inactuel*, Spring 1994.

"Althusser, Don Quixote and the Stage of the Text" was published in an earlier version in the volume edited by Sylvain Lazarus, *Philosophie et politique dans l'oeuvre de Louis Althusser*, Paris: Presses Universitaires de France, 1993.

"Deleuze, Bartleby, and the Literary Formula" was written in response to requests from Jean-Clet Martin, Françoise Proust, and Éric Alliez.

All the above texts have been rewritten for the present book.

# Notes

## "The Excursions of the Word"

1. I have studied the complex relationships of literature with its own idea in *La parole muette. Essai sur les contradictions de la littérature* [Silent speech: Essay on the contradictions of literature], Paris: Hachette, 1998.

## "From Wordsworth to Mandelstam: The Transports of Liberty"

1. See especially the discussion of this question in Gérard Genette, *Introduction à l'architexte*, Paris: Le Seuil, 1979.

2. *Cf.* Jacques Rancière, *Courts voyages au pays du peuple*, Paris: Le Seuil, 1990. [Translated as *Short Voyages to the Land of the People* by James Swenson, Stanford: Stanford University Press, 2003.]

3. Wordsworth, preface to the *Lyrical Ballads*, in *William Wordsworth*, The Oxford Authors, Oxford University Press, 1984, p. 597.

4. *Cf.*, especially, "The Nineteenth Century," in Osip Mandelstam, *On Poetry*. [Translated into English by Sidney Monas in *Selected Essays*, Austin: University of Texas Press, 1977, pp. 94–100.]

5. *Cf.* the poem "To Cassandra" and also the essay "Pushkin and Scriabin" [in *Selected Essays, op. cit.*, p. 123]. For the identification of the "Sun of Alexander" with the "nocturnal sun of Pushkin," see the interpretation by Steven Broyde, *Osip Mandelstam and His Age*, Cambridge: Harvard University Press, 1975, disputed by Nikita Struve, *Ossip Mandelstam*, Paris: Institut d'études slaves, 1982.

6. "On the Nature of the Word." [*Cf. Selected Essays*, p. 76.]

7. "Word and Culture." [*Cf.* p. 52.]

8. "On the Nature of the Word." [*Cf.* p. 76.]

9. "Word and Culture." [*Cf.* p. 52.]

10. *Ibid.*

11. "On the Nature of the Word." [*Cf.* p. 68.]

12. "On the Nature of the Word." [*Cf.* p. 75.]

13. Mallarmé, "Catholicisme," *Oeuvres complètes* [Complete works], Paris: Gallimard, 1945, p. 393.

### "Rimbaud: Voices and Bodies"

1. On the theme of "charity," its power greater than language and knowledge, its dependency upon the Savior and the disposition of the heart proper to it, see Saint Paul, *I Corinthians*, 13, 8, and *I Timothy*, I, 5.

2. Yves Bonnefoy, "Madame Rimbaud," in *Études sur les "Poésies" de Rimbaud* [Studies on the "Poetries" of Rimbaud] (Marc Eigeldinger, ed.), Neufchâtel: La Baconnière, 1979, pp. 9–43.

### "The Body of the Letter: Bible, Epic, Novel"

1. Erich Auerbach, *Mimesis*, Paris: Gallimard, 1987, p. 59. [Translated into English as *Mimesis: The Representation of Reality in Western Literature* by Willard Trask, New York: Doubleday, 1957. Trask's version of this passage is on p. 41.—Trans.]

2. I am aware here of blurring the distinctions of interpreters who ordinarily use "figurative" in the other sense. But it seems to me more logical to reserve the common term for the common idea.

3. [A character in Balzac's novel] *Le Curé de village* analyzed in the chapter "Balzac and the Island of the Book," below.

### "Proust: War, Truth, Book"

1. "Letter to Gaston Gallimard, May 1916," *Correspondence*, Paris: Gallimard, Vol. XV, p. 132.

2. *La Recherche du temps perdu*, III, p. 982.

3. *Op. cit.*, pp. 776.

4. *Op. cit.*, pp. 770–71.

5. *Op. cit.*, pp. 752–53.

6. *Op. cit.*, p. 151.

7. *Op. cit.*, I, p. 151.

8. *Op. cit.*, III, p. 774.

9. Maurice Barrès, "Le coeur des femmes de France" [The heart of the women of France], *Chronique de la grande guerre* [Chronicle of the Great War], p. 151.

10. *Op. cit.*, p. 866.

*"Althusser, Don Quixote, and the Stage of the Text"*

1. The "very grave conflict that is our present drama" is the Sino-Soviet conflict and the development of a Maoist protest against the [Moscow] line of the French Communist Party.

*"Deleuze, Bartleby, and the Literary Formula"*

1. Gilles Deleuze, "Bartleby ou la formule" [Bartleby or the formula], in *Critique et clinique*, Paris: Minuit, 1993, pp. 89–114. [Translated as *Essays Critical and Clinical* by Daniel W. Smith and Michael A. Greco, Minneapolis: University of Minnesota Press, 1997.]

2. Letter from Flaubert to Louise Colet, January 16, 1852.

3. "Crise de vers," *Oeuvres complètes*, Paris: Gallimard, 1945, p. 364.

4. Gustave Flaubert, *La Tentation de saint Antoine* [The temptation of Saint Anthony], Paris: Louis Conard, 1924, p. 418.

5. *Ibid.*, p. 417.

6. Gilles Deleuze, *Mille plateaux*, Paris: Minuit, 1980, p. 343. Translated as *A Thousand Plateaus: Capitalism and Schizophrenia* by Brian Massumi, London: Athlone Press, 1988.

7. Letter from Flaubert to Louise Colet, January 16, 1852.

8. Letter from Flaubert to Louise Colet, February 1, 1852.

9. "What is discovered is the world where people do not speak, the silent vegetable world, the madness of Flowers [ . . . ]," Gilles Deleuze, *Proust et les signes*, Paris: Presses universitaires de France, 1993, p. 210. [Translated as *Proust and Signs: The Complete Text* by Richard Howard, Minneapolis: University of Minnesota Press, 2000.]

10. Marcel Proust, "A propos du style de Flaubert" [On the subject of Flaubert's style], in *Contre Sainte-Beuve*, Paris: Gallimard, 1971, p. 587. [Translated as *Against Sainte-Beuve and Other Essays* by John Sturrock, New York : Penguin Books, 1988.]

11. *Cf.* the text, "Présence et fonction de la folie, l'Araignée" [Presence and function of madness, the Spider], that serves as conclusion to the last version of *Proust et les signes*.

12. Gilles Deleuze, *Critique et clinique*, Paris: Minuit, 1993, p. 94.

13. *Op. cit.*, p. 106.

14. *Ibid.*

15. Letter from Flaubert to Louise Colet, May 26, 1853.

16. It is in this sense that Proust contrasts it to friendship in a letter to Emmanuel Berl in 1916, which refers explicitly to Schopenhauer. *Correspondance*, Paris: Gallimard, Vol. XV, pp. 26–28.

17. Gilles Deleuze, *L'Image-temps*, Paris: Minuit, 1985, p. 196. [Translated as *The Time Image* by Hugh Tomlinson and Robert Galeta, Minneapolis: University of Minnesota Press, 1989.] I thank Raymond Bellour for drawing my attention to the importance of this text by making it the topic of a program at the États généraux du documentaire in Lussas, 1997.

18. *Op. cit.*, p. 197.

19. *Critique et clinique*, p. 114.

20. *Op. cit.*, p. 110. [*Cf.* p. 86 in the English—Trans.]

21. I'm borrowing this expression from "L'Introduction à la mystique du cinéma" by the great Nietzschean Élie Faure, while making reference here to the interpretation of Deleuze's thinking by Alain Badiou, *Deleuze: La clameur de l'être*, Paris: Hachette, 1997. [Translated as *Deleuze: The Clamor of Being* by Louise Burchill, Minneapolis: University of Minnesota Press, 2000.]

UNIVERSITY OF WINCHESTER
LIBRARY

UNIVERSITY OF WINCHESTER
LIBRARY